CUPCAKES
GALORE

CUPCAKES
GALORE

GAIL WAGMAN

Bounty
Books

First published in Great Britain in 2006
by MQ Publications Limited

This edition published in 2010 by Bounty Books,
a division of Octopus Publishing Group Ltd
Endeavour House, 189 Shaftesbury Avenue,
London, WC2H 8JY
www.octopusbooks.co.uk

An Hachette UK Company
www.hachette.co.uk

Copyright © Octopus Publishing Group Ltd
      2006, 2008
Text copyright © Gail Wagman 2006

Gail Wagman asserts the moral right to be
identified as the author of this book.

Photography: Olivier Maynard
Design: Clare Barber

ISBN: 978-0-753720-17-2

A CIP catalogue record of this book is available
from the British Library.

Printed and bound in China

CONTENTS

Introduction 6

Grandma's Favourites 16

Kids' Cupcakes 40

After Dinner Cupcakes 60

Gourmet Cupcakes 82

Holiday Cupcakes 118

Cupcakes Plus 146

Index 186

INTRODUCTION

When the idea of writing a book on cupcakes was first broached to me, I immediately had visions of those cupcakes of my youth – the ones my mother used to make for the birthday parties of my childhood.

You remember – they were usually made with either chocolate or yellow batter, lavished with gobs of pastel icing and decorated with chocolate sprinkles, coconut, candied fruits or nuts. They were always served on a big platter with a candle in each one in honour of the birthday girl or boy or brought to school on that special day to be shared with friends during break-

time. Cupcakes have of course come a long way since then, thanks to the amazing amount of cupcake paraphernalia available on the market, from decorations to cupcake tins, as well as the many recipes expressly designed for them or that can be adapted to them. But we will come back to that later. For the time being, let's set the record straight. Just what is a cupcake? And what isn't? Webster's Dictionary defines a cupcake as follows:

noun:

a small cake baked in a cuplike mould

This minimal definition just about sums it up – no more, no less – leaving a great deal of room for interpretation, creativity and perhaps a little confusion.

★ A CUPCAKE WITH ANY OTHER NAME ... ★

A cupcake is undeniably a 'little cake,' but all 'little cakes' aren't necessarily cupcakes. Unless they are made in a cup-sized mould. And fit the criteria of a 'cake,' let's say, as opposed to a muffin, which can be made in a cup-sized mould but is basically a quick bread and not a cake. And then again, some cupcake recipes are 'quick' but the result is not to be mistaken for a muffin. And does a cupcake require icing to conform to the appellation? Iconographically speaking, I would say yes since the festive character of the beast certainly lends itself to a little 'dressing up for the occasion,' but it would really be too bad to add anything other than icing sugar or a little glaze to some of the cupcakes in this book. A number of sources refer to the origin of the humble cupcake as a 'cup cake,' in other words, a 1 cup butter–2 cups sugar–3 cups flour –4 eggs cake, which can certainly be made into cupcakes (provided that you add a little flavouring, a substantial dose of imagination, some yummy icing and a decoration or two) but as anyone who has ever made a cake will know, this refers to what is commonly known as a pound cake and no one is mistaking that for a cupcake.

So, if you stick to my definition, you can't go wrong. Just remember the three cardinal rules:

1. cupcakes should be pretty
2. cupcakes should taste good
3. cupcakes should be fun.

★ THE PARTY BEAST ★

Defining a cupcake is sort of like defining a pair of shorts (or short pants). Or a can of fizzy drink (compared to a bottle). Or a bikini (as opposed to a one-piece swimming costume). It is just a smaller version of the original that has taken on a meaning of its own (thus the confusion). When referring to cupcakes, most of the respectable cookbooks that I have consulted agree that nearly all cake batters lend themselves to being baked in individual portions. My experience has certainly proved that to be true. It is a rare cake batter that cannot be metamorphosed into a cupcake with the addition of some sort of topping or decoration. So I have decided to stick with my original idea of the cupcake as a 'party beast' – no 'savoury' cupcakes here – I'll leave that for the muffin department. My two basic criteria were (1) the cupcakes all had to be made with some sort of cake batter (to be defined); and (2) they could be made in a cupcake tin – either with or without a paper, mini, regular or jumbo. I have added an extra section entitled

'Cupcakes Plus' for those 'cupcakes' that may or may not specifically fit those criteria but that can be made in a cupcake tin and/or served in a cupcake paper and that could pass for a cupcake with a little imagination.

I hope you enjoy these recipes. I had great fun writing them and am very excited about sharing them with you. Special thanks to my 'testers' – Mark, my son, and his friends at school who received a batch every Monday morning to start off the week; Brigitte and Christian who stopped by on Saturday mornings after the market to try my latest creations and whose detailed tasting notes were invaluable; and to all my other friends who have been on a 'cupcake diet' since I started this project. I am forever grateful to Alain, my partner in all culinary endeavours, for having not only tested all of my recipes but for having so patiently listened to the 'Cupcake Monologue' during the gestation of this book. And then there is of course my daughter Emily who could leave no cupcake paper unturned and who constantly supplied me with ideas and cupcake paraphernalia while I was writing the book.

SOME RULES
of Thumb

Here are a few helpful hints for the aspiring cupcake baker. So put on that apron and get to work!

★ RECIPES ★

Almost all of the cupcake recipes in this book (with the exception of some of the ones in the 'Cupcakes Plus' section) are really cake recipes tailored to a cupcake. As I already mentioned in the introduction, just about any cake recipe can be used to make a cupcake. Only the cooking time will change which is true within the range of cupcake sizes as well – mini cupcakes will take less time than regular cupcakes that will take less time than jumbo cupcakes that will take less time than a cake. Logical, isn't it? Take your favourite cake recipe, bake it in a cupcake tin, add a little icing, a glaze, some icing sugar and a decoration, and you will have your own original cupcake recipe. Let your imagination be your guide.

★ INGREDIENTS ★

As a rule of thumb, all ingredients should be at room temperature unless otherwise indicated (frozen berries, hot milk, etc.). I used plain flour for all of the recipes in this book. I never use self-raising flour since it already has salt and a leavening agent in it and I prefer to add my own. As for leavening agents, I generally use 1 teaspoon baking powder per 150g flour and fraction thereof. I only use bicarbonate of soda when there is an acid factor such as buttermilk, soured cream, yogurt or citrus juice. Otherwise, it apparently serves no purpose. Whenever possible, I mix all of the dry ingredients together before mixing them into the batter. Which brings us to the question – to sieve or not to sieve? From all that I have read and from my own experience, I don't think sieving adds anything to a recipe except when you are adding small quantities of flour to beaten egg whites with a whisk, allowing you to add the flour slowly and not to deflate the whites. In my old recipe books from the 50s, ingredients are sometimes sieved three times before being measured. I'm not sure what the logic was but I wouldn't waste my time.

I only use unsalted butter. I live in France and almost all of the butter available is unsalted. If you are using salted butter, leave the salt out of the recipe. Both salt and cream of tartar are used to stabilize beaten egg whites. Use about $\frac{1}{8}$ teaspoon cream of tartar or a pinch of salt for every 2 egg whites.

★ BAKING TIPS ★

Most of the recipes call for the cupcake papers or moulds to be filled $\frac{2}{3}$ full. There are exceptions of course. If you are adding a topping, you may want to leave more room (Strawberry-Filled Oatmeal Cupcake, for instance). Unless otherwise stated, I generally suggest preheating the oven to 180°C/350°F/Gas Mark 4. Some recipes require a hotter or a cooler oven and, occasionally, the temperature has to be turned down while the cupcakes are baking. In that case, just follow the recipe. I tend to bake just about everything in a moderate, preheated oven. Remember that temperatures vary from one oven to the next, so know your oven and use your common sense. There are just so many variables — weather, altitude, position in the oven, whether it is a first or second batch, etc. I usually insert a tester in my cupcakes to see if they are done. When it comes out clean, remove the cupcakes from the oven. Some cupcakes stay moist in the centre (Chocolate Mousse or cupcakes cooked with fruit like the Blueberry and Raspberry Cream Cupcake for the Fourth of July), defying the 'tester' test. In any case, when they start to burn, regardless of the recipe, you will know that you have left them in the oven too long!

It is generally advisable to let the cupcakes cool before removing them from the tins. Place them on a wire rack when you take them out of the oven. Some can be unmoulded after about 10 minutes whereas the denser ones should be completely cooled first.

Just remember, any rule that applies to cake baking techniques or ingredients generally applies to cupcakes.

EQUIPMENT

Cupcake paraphernalia can be found in just about any supermarket and in all good kitchen supply stores.

★ CUPCAKE TINS ★

Cupcake tins (also known as muffin tins) come in a variety of sizes but the three major sizes are 'mini' (3 to 5cm in diameter, holding 30ml or 2 tablespoons batter), 'regular' (7cm diameter, holding 60 to 80ml batter), and 'jumbo' (8.5cm in diameter, holding about 150ml batter). The number of cups in the tin is variable. I have mini-cupcake tins with 20 cups and others with 30. There are usually 12 cups in a regular-size cupcake tin whereas the silicone ones are often smaller. My jumbo tins make six jumbo cupcakes each. Tins come in metal, in which case you have to grease and flour them if you are not using cupcake papers. Although I see no reason not to use cupcake papers and avoid the mess. The new silicone moulds are very handy and can be used at high temperatures in an oven without any additional preparation. They are non-stick

and the cupcakes will just pop out as soon as they are cool. They come in rigid and non-rigid varieties and are extremely easy to clean. Just remember to use a baking sheet with the non-rigid ones. I prefer metal tins when using cupcake papers and non-stick silicone moulds when I am not.

★ CUPCAKE PAPERS ★

Cupcake papers come in a variety of colours and designs. I have found ones for just about every occasion – Christmas, Valentine's Day, Halloween, St. Patrick's Day, etc. and for every season – autumn leaves and spring flowers, just to name a few. There are papers with Barbie dolls, hearts, footballs, and some rather unidentifiable objects. Supermarkets seem to carry the pastel ones of my youth whereas many of the speciality stores carry plain white ones which are good

for any occasion. They also come in a full rainbow of colours and in gold and silver. The variety is slightly more limited for the mini and jumbo versions. And plain papers will do just fine. Remember, it is what is inside and on top that counts.

As for any other equipment you will need to make a cupcake, it is basically the same as what you would need to make a cake – spatula, whisk, wooden spoon, measuring cups and spoons, electric or hand beater, electric mixer and a wide range of bowl sizes. You will also need some equipment to make icings and decorations, but I will cover that in the section devoted to those topics.

DRESSING UP FOR
the Occasion

Icings, frosting, toppings and glazes and, last but not least, decorations.

★ THE CROWNING TOUCH ★

Is a cupcake a cupcake with nothing on top? Since I'm not quite sure but tend to believe that a cupcake is the sum of its individual parts, I have given at least one alternative for every cupcake in this book — whether it be an icing or frosting as in the majority of the recipes, a topping as in the case of the Apple Crumble or Bourdaloue, a glaze for the Kir or Honey Hazelnut Cupcake, or just a dusting of icing sugar for the Poppyseed Cupcake — plus some sort of decoration.

I have used the terms 'frosting' and 'icing' interchangeably. Webster's Dictionary gives 'icing' as a synonym for 'frosting' and vice versa. I just love the definition of 'icing' in my Webster's Dictionary and you will see why: 'a sweet, flavoured and usually creamy mixture used to coat baked goods (as cupcakes) [sic] — called also frosting.' Can you believe that? So I guess that cupcakes are just predestined to have some sort of icing/frosting/topping/glaze. After all, they could have said 'cakes.' But no. They explicitly mention cupcakes. In Alan Davidson's *Oxford Companion to Food*, he goes into great detail about 'icings' but doesn't mention 'frosting.' The *Joy of Cooking* has a whole section on 'Icings' whereas the *Fanny Farmer Cookbook* has it all under 'Frostings.'

Cake/cupcake icing/frosting is an art in itself. As is cake/cupcake decorating. Many books exist on the subject and all good cookbooks will have a section devoted to the topic as well. I have tried to present a full panoply of alternatives, from the simple to the more complicated – easy-to-make-icings with just icing sugar and a little liquid, to cooked icings that require a bit more skill and time. Ready-made icings can be found in supermarkets and speciality stores if you are in a hurry although some of the recipes in this book can be made in the time it will take you to open the tin or read the directions on the ready-made stuff. Fondant is a challenge to even the most skilled baker and I always use one of the brands available on the market, with the addition of a little sugar syrup, flavouring and colouring, if need may be. Feel free to mix and match as well. And create your own personalized versions by changing the flavours. For example, replace the mint in the Mint Butter Cream Frosting with lavender or lemon extract, or a few drops of orange flower water or rose water, and invent your own recipes. A little imagination will go a long way.

And speaking of imagination – a word on cupcake decorations! I guess you could just say 'awesome.' On a recent trip to the States, I was astounded and impressed by the quantity of decorations available on the market. I mean, there is just no excuse for an ugly cupcake at this point in civilization. Glitter sugars, coloured sugars, every shape and size of sprinkles for every occasion, instant decorator tubes in every colour of the rainbow, coloured sprays, edible decorations in the form of flowers, clowns, footballs – you name it – plus all the rest including dried and jellied fruits, nuts, gummy sweets, miniature sweets and cookies – and those are just some of the obvious ones. So, in the spirit of that party beast known as the cupcake – free your inner 'cupcake decorator' – and have a ball.

GRANDMA'S
FAVOURITES

COURGETTE PINE NUT
Cupcakes

This is one way of using up some of that extra courgette and getting your kids to eat it too. They'll never know but they will surely ask for seconds. And it will be a great hit with adults as well.

MAKES: **ABOUT 12–14 CUPCAKES**

100g grated courgette
200g plain flour
2 teaspoons baking powder
1 teaspoon salt
100g ground almonds
1 egg
130g sugar
160ml double cream
80ml vegetable oil
100g pine nuts

CREAM CHEESE FROSTING
150g icing sugar
120g cream cheese, softened
1 egg white, slightly beaten
Pinch of salt
1 teaspoon vanilla extract
100g pine nuts for decoration

1. Preheat oven to 180°C/350°F/Gas Mark 4.

2. In a large bowl, mix together courgette, flour, baking powder, salt and ground almonds.

3. In another bowl, mix the egg, sugar, cream, oil and pine nuts. Pour this batter into the first one and blend well with a whisk or a wooden spoon.

4. Fill cupcake papers about ¾ full and cook for 20–25 minutes or until a tester inserted into the centre comes out clean. Remove from the oven and cool.

5. Beat all the frosting ingredients together until light and of good spreading consistency. Frost the cooled cupcakes and sprinkle a few pine nuts over each cupcake before serving. Alternatively, dust the cooled cupcakes with icing sugar.

CUPCAKE TIP
If you don't have pine nuts, use either walnuts or hazelnuts.

CHOCOLATE COCONUT
Cupcakes

Instant chocolate pudding was a staple of my childhood. My mother would make it as a special treat, to be eaten slowly, treasuring every mouthful. These cupcakes are a tribute to that time long ago and the coconut is my little personal touch.

MAKES: ABOUT 12–14 CUPCAKES

250g plain flour
2 teaspoons baking powder
1 teaspoon salt, plus pinch for egg
    whites
3 eggs, separated
100g soft brown sugar
125ml vegetable oil, plus
    2 tablespoons
100g desiccated coconut, plus
    2 tablespoons for dusting
2 tablespoons cocoa powder
120g dark chocolate, grated
4 tablespoons milk
Chocolate pudding (instant, ready-
    made or homemade)
Whipped cream, for decoration
Powdered chocolate or cocoa powder
    for dusting

1. Preheat oven to 180°C/350°F/Gas Mark 4.

2. Mix flour, baking powder and salt and set aside.

3. With a whisk or a wooden spoon, mix egg yolks and sugar together. Add oil and then flour mixture, beating until batter is smooth. Mix in coconut, cocoa powder, grated chocolate and milk and blend well.

4. Using an electric beater, beat egg whites with a pinch of salt until stiff but not dry. Gently fold into chocolate batter.

5. Spoon batter into cupcake papers, filling about ⅔ full. Smooth batter with the back of a spoon. Sprinkle a little coconut over each cupcake. Cook for 10 minutes and then lower temperature to 150°C/300°F/Gas Mark 2 and cook for another 20 minutes or until a tester inserted into the centre comes out clean. Remove from oven and cool.

6. When cupcakes are completely cool, cut a circle or cone out of the top with an apple corer and heap chocolate pudding in it. Add a little dollop of whipped cream for decoration. Dust with powdered chocolate or cocoa powder.

BLACK & WHITE
Cupcakes

Native New Yorkers will be familiar with these cupcakes although they are traditionally found in cookie form at delicatessens throughout America.

MAKES: ABOUT 16 CUPCAKES

CHOCOLATE & VANILLA
MARBLE CUPCAKE
225g plain flour
2 teaspoons baking powder
1 teaspoon salt, plus pinch for the
    egg whites
180g unsalted butter, room
    temperature
200g sugar
2 eggs, separated
80ml full-fat milk
1 teaspoon vanilla extract
1 tablespoon cocoa powder

BLACK & WHITE ICING
300g icing sugar
60ml boiling water (more or less,
    depending on spreading
    consistency)
30g dark chocolate
Chocolate buttons for decoration

1. Preheat oven to 180°C/350°F/Gas Mark 4. Mix dry ingredients together in a bowl. Set aside.

2. In the large bowl of an electric mixer, cream butter and sugar until light and fluffy. Add egg yolks and beat to blend. Alternately add dry ingredients and milk, beating well after each addition. Divide batter into two separate bowls. Mix the vanilla into one of the batters and cocoa into the other.

3. Beat egg whites with a pinch of salt until they form stiff peaks. Divide in half and gently fold half into each of the two batters.

4. Spoon batter into cupcake papers, filling cups about $2/3$ full, 1 heaped teaspoon at a time, alternating batters. They will appear not to be mixed but will 'marble' when cooked. Bake for 25 minutes or until a tester inserted into the centre comes out clean. Remove from oven and cool.

5. To make the icing: place icing sugar in a medium-size bowl. Gradually mix in boiling water, 1 tablespoon at a time. Mixture should be very thick but easy to spread. Divide mixture into two parts.

6. Put half the icing in a double boiler with the chocolate over simmering (not boiling) water. Stir and remove from heat as soon as the chocolate is melted. While icing is warm to the touch, spread on cupcakes – half white, half chocolate. Place a chocolate button in the centre of each cupcake.

BLUE BLUEBERRY 'N' CREAM Cupcakes

The 'trick,' for these cupcakes is to defrost the blueberries until they became mushy so that they impart their blue colour to the batter.

MAKES: ABOUT 18 REGULAR CUPCAKES OR 8 JUMBO CUPCAKES

375g plain flour
3 teaspoons baking powder
1 teaspoon salt
125g unsalted butter, room temperature
200g sugar
2 eggs
240ml milk or single cream
135g blueberries (if you are using frozen blueberries, defrost beforehand), plus 90g frozen or fresh blueberries
1 tablespoon water

BLUE BLUEBERRY WHIPPED CREAM
240ml whipping cream
50g sugar
45g reserved crushed blueberries (see method)
Dried blueberries (optional) for decoration

1. Preheat oven to 180°C/350°F/Gas Mark 4. Mix flour, baking powder and salt together and set aside.

2. In the large bowl of an electric mixer, cream butter and sugar until light and fluffy. Add eggs, one at a time, beating well after each addition. Alternately add dry ingredients and milk or cream.

3. Using a fork, crush 135g blueberries with 1 tablespoon water until they are soft. Save 45g for the whipped cream. Add 90g to the batter and blend thoroughly. Batter will be blue. Gently fold in remaining 90g blueberries.

4. Spoon batter into cupcake papers, filling cups about 2/3 full. Cook for 20–25 minutes or until a tester inserted into the centre comes out clean. Remove from oven and cool.

5. To make the whipped cream: with an electric beater, beat cream until it starts to form soft peaks. Gradually add sugar, beating constantly. Add reserved crushed blueberries and beat until stiff.

6. Top cupcakes with whipped cream and sprinkle with dried blueberries, if desired. These cupcakes should be iced just before serving. Alternatively, because of their beautiful colour, you can leave them as is and dust them with icing sugar.

BROWNIE Cupcakes

This recipe is dedicated to Julien, who is my biggest brownie fan, no matter what form they come in!

MAKES: ABOUT 12 CUPCAKES

150g plain flour
1 teaspoon baking powder
1 teaspoon salt
180g dark chocolate, broken
    into pieces
80g unsalted butter, room
    temperature, cut into pieces
150g sugar
2 eggs
1 teaspoon vanilla extract
100g chopped walnuts

WALNUT FUDGE FROSTING
90g dark chocolate, cut
    into pieces
200g sugar
80ml milk
3 tablespoons unsalted butter
1 tablespoon golden syrup
Pinch of salt
1 teaspoon vanilla extract

FOR DECORATION
50g chopped walnuts (optional) or
    12 walnut halves
Chocolate buttons

1. Preheat oven to 180°C/350°F/Gas Mark 4.

2. Mix flour, baking powder and salt together and set aside.

3. Place chocolate, butter and sugar in a large bowl over simmering water. Heat until just melted, stirring from time to time (do not cook). This will only take a few minutes. Remove from heat. Add eggs, one at a time, blending well after each addition. Add vanilla. Gradually add dry ingredients. When batter is smooth and dry ingredients have been absorbed, fold in chopped walnuts.

4. Divide batter between 12 cupcake papers, smoothing with the back of a spoon. Cook for about 20–25 minutes. Cupcakes should form a crust on top and be a little moist inside. Remove from oven and cool completely before removing from tin.

5. To make the frosting: place all of the ingredients except the vanilla and walnuts in a heavy saucepan. Bring to the boil and cook for 1 minute, stirring constantly. Remove from heat and cool (you can set bowl in cold water to speed up the process).

6. Add vanilla and beat until thick, about 10 minutes, until frosting is fluffy and the colour has slightly lightened. If you are using chopped walnuts in the frosting, fold them in now. Frost cooled cupcakes. Top each cupcake with walnut halves and a chocolate button.

CHOCOLATE PEANUT BUTTER Cupcakes

Peanut butter and chocolate are one of those fabulous duos, immortalized in many children's candies and traditional desserts.

MAKES: ABOUT 18 CUPCAKES

300g plain flour
2 teaspoons baking powder
1 teaspoon salt
60g good quality dark chocolate
60g unsalted butter, room temperature
4 tablespoons smooth peanut butter
200g sugar
2 eggs
180ml milk
120g peanut chocolate chips (optional)

FROSTING

90g milk chocolate
60g unsalted butter, cut into small pieces
250g icing sugar
Pinch of salt
60ml double cream
1 teaspoon vanilla extract
3 tablespoons smooth peanut butter
Peanut-chocolate sweets (peanut M&M's, Reese's Pieces etc.)

1. Preheat oven to 180°C/350°F/Gas Mark 4.

2. Mix flour, baking powder and salt together and set aside.

3. Melt chocolate in a large bowl over simmering water. Set aside to cool.

4. In the large bowl of an electric mixer, cream butter, peanut butter and sugar until light and fluffy. Add eggs, one at a time, mixing well after each addition. Add cooled chocolate and blend well. Alternately beat in dry ingredients and milk.

5. Spoon batter into cupcake papers, filling cups about ⅔ full. Sprinkle a few peanut chocolate chips over each cupcake, gently pressing them into the batter with a fork. Bake for 25 minutes or until a tester comes out clean. Remove from oven and cool.

6. To make the frosting: heat chocolate and butter in a large bowl over simmering water until just melted. Remove from heat and cool.

7. Using a whisk or a wooden spoon, beat sugar, salt, cream and vanilla until smooth. Add cooled chocolate mixture and peanut butter and beat until blended. Put the frosting in the refrigerator until it thickens (about 20–30 minutes).

8. Remove from refrigerator, beat until frosting is of spreading consistency and frost cooled cupcakes. Decorate with peanut-chocolate sweets.

LEMON MERINGUE PIE Cupcakes

These lemon meringue cupcakes will add an elegant touch to the end of any meal. Lemon desserts are always a favourite because of their tart flavour. Add this one to your repertory.

MAKES: ABOUT 12 CUPCAKES

225g plain flour
2 teaspoons baking powder
1 teaspoon salt
2 tablespoons grated lemon rind
125g unsalted butter
200g sugar
2 eggs
2 tablespoons lemon juice

LEMON CREAM

150g sugar
3 tablespoons plain flour
Pinch of salt
60ml lemon juice
Grated rind of 1 lemon
120ml water
3 egg yolks, beaten (save whites for meringue)
65g unsalted butter

MERINGUE TOPPING

3 egg whites
Pinch of salt
50g sugar
A few teaspoons of sugar for dusting

1. Prepare the lemon cream. In a large bowl mix sugar, flour and salt together. Add lemon juice and rind. Mix well. Beat in water, egg yolks and butter (if the butter is still chunky it will melt over the hot water).

2. Place bowl over a saucepan of hot simmering water and cook until smooth and thick, stirring constantly with a whisk (about 20 minutes). Cool and set aside. Preheat oven to 180°C/350°F/Gas Mark 4.

3. Mix flour, baking powder, salt and lemon rind together. Set aside.

4. Cream butter and sugar together until light and fluffy. Add eggs, one at a time, beating after each addition. Add lemon juice and beat until well blended. Add flour mixture and continue beating until batter is smooth.

5. Fill 12 cupcake papers with the batter. Cook for 15 minutes or until cupcakes are golden on top. Remove from oven and cool for 10 minutes.

6. To make the meringue: beat egg whites with a pinch of salt until they start to stiffen. Gradually add sugar, beating until stiff but not dry.

7. Using a sharp knife, carefully remove a little cone from the centre of the cooled cupcakes using an apple corer and fill with lemon cream.

8. Place 1 tablespoon meringue on each cupcake, forming peaks with the back of a spoon or a fork. Dust lightly with sugar. Cook cupcakes in the oven for another 5–7 minutes or until meringue is just golden. Leave to cool.

APPLE-CRANBERRY CRUMBLE Cupcakes

These moist cupcakes will remind you of the homemade crumbles you ate when you were a kid. The cranberries give a slightly tart taste and a beautiful colour.

MAKES: ABOUT 18 CUPCAKES

225g plain flour
2 teaspoons baking powder
1 teaspoon salt
2 teaspoons cinnamon
½ teaspoon grated nutmeg
375g unsalted butter, room temperature
300g sugar
2 eggs
240ml apple sauce (you can either use ready-made or recipe on page 134)
1 tablespoon finely grated lemon rind
200g cranberries (fresh or frozen)
65g walnuts, chopped (optional)

APPLE-WALNUT CRUMBLE TOPPING
30g unsalted butter
6 teaspoons sugar
50g plain flour
1 apple, peeled and cut into small pieces
65g walnuts, chopped

1. Preheat oven to 180°C/350°F/Gas Mark 4.

2. Mix dry ingredients and spices together and set aside.

3. In the large bowl of an electric mixer, cream butter and sugar until light and fluffy. Add eggs, one at a time, beating well after each addition. Alternately add dry ingredients, apple sauce and lemon rind and blend well. Fold in cranberries and walnuts, if desired. If you are using frozen cranberries, don't defrost them beforehand.

4. Spoon batter into cupcake papers, filling cups a little over ½ full. Smooth batter with the back of a spoon.

5. For topping, melt butter in a pan, and add sugar, flour, apple and walnuts. Mix well and stir until mixture just starts to change colour. Remove from heat. Place a spoonful of the mixture on top of each cupcake. Cook cupcakes for about 20 minutes or until a tester inserted into the centre comes out clean. Remove from oven and cool completely before removing cupcakes from tin.

CUPCAKE TIP
Serve these cupcakes with a dollop of whipped cream on top.

MAPLE WALNUT DELIGHTS

These cupcakes are a true gourmet delight. The icing is a good example of cooked frosting at its best – it is both beautiful to look at and will melt in your mouth.

MAKES: ABOUT 18 CUPCAKES

375g plain flour
3 teaspoons baking powder
½ teaspoon salt
125g unsalted butter, room temperature
100g soft light brown sugar
2 eggs
240ml maple syrup
120ml milk
65g chopped walnuts

MAPLE MERINGUE ICING
2 egg whites
Pinch of salt
240ml maple syrup
1 teaspoon vanilla extract
65g chopped walnuts or walnut halves (for decoration)

1. Preheat oven to 180°C/350°F/Gas Mark 4.

2. Mix flour, baking powder and salt together and set aside.

3. In the large bowl of an electric mixer, cream butter and sugar until light and fluffy. Add eggs, one at a time, mixing well after each addition. Alternately add dry ingredients, syrup and milk, blending well after each addition. Fold in walnuts.

4. Spoon batter into cupcake papers, filling cups about ⅔ full. Bake for 25–30 minutes or until a tester inserted into the centre comes out clean. Remove from oven and cool.

5. To make the icing: beat egg whites with a pinch of salt until peaks start to form. Set aside.

6. Boil maple syrup until it forms a soft ball when dropped into a glass of water (about 120°C/234°F on a sugar thermometer). The time will depend on the maple syrup you are using but should be about 5–10 minutes. Remove from heat immediately. Slowly pour the hot syrup into the egg whites, beating constantly. The hot syrup actually cooks the egg whites. Add vanilla and continue beating until mixture is stiff and stands in soft peaks.

7. Ice the cooled cupcakes, forming peaks with the back of a spoon or a fork. Place a walnut half on top of each cupcake or sprinkle with chopped walnuts before icing hardens. It will harden on the outside and remain soft and creamy inside.

THREE-GINGERBREAD Cupcakes

The fresh and crystallized ginger give these cupcakes a unique and very pronounced flavour. Enjoy with a cup of strong black tea or an espresso.

MAKES: ABOUT 12 CUPCAKES

225g plain flour
2 teaspoons baking powder
1 teaspoon salt
1 teaspoon ground ginger
½ teaspoon cinnamon
½ teaspoon allspice
Dash each of grated nutmeg and
  ground cloves
125g unsalted butter, room
  temperature
150g soft brown sugar
2 eggs
1 teaspoon vanilla extract
1 heaping tablespoon grated ginger
120ml milk
3 tablespoons finely chopped
  crystallized ginger

GINGER CREAM FROSTING
120ml whipping cream, chilled
4 tablespoons sugar
½ teaspoon ground ginger
1 teaspoon finely grated fresh ginger
Sliced crystallized ginger for decoration

1. Preheat oven to 180°C/350°F/Gas Mark 4.

2. Mix flour, baking powder, salt and spices together and set aside.

3. In the large bowl of an electric mixer, cream butter and sugar until light and fluffy. Add eggs, one at a time, mixing well after each addition. Add vanilla and grated ginger. Alternately add dry ingredients and milk, beating continually. When batter is smooth, fold in crystallized ginger.

4. Spoon batter into cupcake papers, filling cups about ⅔ full. Bake for 20–25 minutes or until a tester inserted in the centre comes out clean. Remove from oven and cool.

5. To make the frosting: whip cream with an electric beater until almost stiff. Gradually add sugar and ground ginger, beating constantly until stiff peaks form. Fold in grated fresh ginger and frost cooled cupcakes. Sprinkle with ground ginger (go easy!) and decorate with a slice of crystallized ginger. These cupcakes have to be frosted just before serving them. They will not keep for long unless you use some sort of fixative for the whipped cream.

CUPCAKE TIP
Alternatively, make a simple glaze by heating a few tablespoons of ginger preserves.

STRAWBERRY-FILLED OATMEAL Cupcakes

These moist and crunchy cupcakes make a delicious dessert or a welcome snack, and if they aren't all gobbled down immediately, they keep well and can be eaten for breakfast.

MAKES: ABOUT 12 CUPCAKES

125g butter, softened
150g plain flour
1 teaspoon baking powder
1 teaspoon bicarbonate of soda
1 teaspoon salt
1 teaspoon cinnamon
75g rolled oats
150g sugar
1 egg
1 teaspoon vanilla extract
240ml soured cream
12 teaspoons strawberry jam

OATMEAL CRUNCH TOPPING
50g rolled oats
50g soft light brown sugar
2 heaped tablespoons plain flour
1 teaspoon cinnamon
½ teaspoon salt
60g unsalted butter, chilled and cut
   into little pieces

1. Put all of the topping ingredients in a food processor and process until lumps form. Set aside.

2. Preheat oven to 180°C/350°F/Gas Mark 4.

3. Mix dry ingredients together and set aside.

4. In the large bowl of an electric mixer, cream butter and sugar until light and fluffy. Add egg and vanilla and mix well. Alternately add dry ingredients and soured cream, blending well after each addition.

5. Spoon half of the batter into 12 cupcake papers. Make an indentation and place 1 teaspoon of jam in each cupcake. Fill cupcakes with remaining batter. Using your fingers, sprinkle a little topping over each cupcake. Cook for 25–30 minutes or until cupcakes are golden brown on top. Remove from oven and cool.

CUPCAKE TIP
*Any type of jam
can be used for
the filling.*

PERSIMMON NUT HARVEST Treats

These cupcakes are a nice alternative to spice cake and a good way to use persimmons.

MAKES: ABOUT 18 CUPCAKES

250g plain flour
2 teaspoons baking powder
1 teaspoon salt
1 teaspoon cinnamon
$\frac{1}{2}$ teaspoon ground ginger
Dash each of grated nutmeg and ground cloves
1 tablespoon grated orange rind
250g unsalted butter
150g granulated sugar
150g soft light brown sugar
1 egg
200g puréed persimmon pulp (about 3 very ripe persimmons)
200g coarsely ground nuts (walnuts, pecans or hazelnuts)

ORANGE CREAM CHEESE FROSTING
240g cream cheese
30g unsalted butter
225g icing sugar
1 teaspoon grated orange rind
2 teaspoons orange juice
Dried persimmons for decoration

1. Preheat oven to 180°C/350°F/Gas Mark 4.

2. Mix all of the dry ingredients together and stir in the orange rind. Set aside.

3. In the large bowl of an electric mixer, cream butter and sugars until light and fluffy. Add egg and beat well. Alternately add flour mixture and persimmon pulp, beating well after each addition. Fold in nuts.

4. Spoon batter into cupcake papers, filling cups about $\frac{2}{3}$ full. Smooth batter with the back of a spoon. Bake for 25 minutes or until a tester inserted into the centre comes out clean. Remove from oven and cool completely before unmoulding.

5. To make the frosting: in a large bowl, mix together cream cheese and butter until smooth and well blended. Gradually add sugar and beat until the mixture is light and fluffy. Beat in the orange rind and juice and place in the refrigerator for about an hour before frosting cooled cupcakes. Top with a piece of dried persimmon.

CUPCAKE TIP
You can substitute lemon for the orange in both the cupcake and the frosting.

STRAWBERRY RHUBARB CRISP Cupcakes

Strawberries and rhubarb go particularly well together. The strawberries seem to bring out the subtle flavour of the rhubarb as well as its colour.

MAKES: ABOUT 16 REGULAR CUPCAKES OR 8 JUMBO CUPCAKES

150g chopped rhubarb, fresh or
    frozen
200g sugar, plus 3 tablespoons if you
    are using fresh rhubarb (see step 1)
200g plain flour
2 teaspoons baking powder
1 teaspoon bicarbonate of soda
1 teaspoon salt
1 teaspoon cinnamon
125g unsalted butter, room
    temperature
2 eggs
1 teaspoon vanilla extract
240ml buttermilk (you can substitute
    milk, in which case you eliminate
    the bicarbonate of soda)

STRAWBERRY GLAZE
115g strawberry jam
175g fresh strawberries, washed,
    cleaned, and cut into quarters
    lengthways, for decoration

1. If you are using fresh rhubarb, wash and peel the rhubarb, cut it into small slices (as you would celery) and place it in a colander in the sink or over a bowl. Sprinkle with 3 tablespoons sugar and leave to drain for half an hour. This will make the rhubarb more tender and will bring out its taste.

2. Preheat oven to 180°C/350°F/Gas Mark 4.

3. Mix flour, baking powder, bicarbonate of soda, salt and cinnamon together and set aside.

4. In the large bowl of an electric mixer, cream butter and sugar until light and fluffy. Add eggs, one at a time, mixing well after each addition. Add vanilla. Alternately add dry ingredients and buttermilk or milk, beating continually. When batter is smooth, fold in rhubarb.

5. Spoon batter into either regular or jumbo cupcake papers, filling about ⅔ full. Bake for 20–25 minutes or until a tester inserted into the centre comes out clean. Remove from oven and cool.

6. Melt strawberry jam over very low heat. When just melted, spread on cooled cupcakes with a pastry brush. Place sliced strawberries in a circle in the centre. Brush a little jam over them so that they will stay in place and take on a glossy sheen.

YOGURT Cupcakes

These very-easy-to-make cupcakes are both healthy and tasty and will make a great snack or an elegant dessert, accompanied by a fresh fruit salad.

MAKES: **ABOUT 18 CUPCAKES**

1 container yogurt (about 125g)
2 containers sugar (about 250g)
3 eggs, lightly beaten
½ container vegetable oil
3 containers plain flour (about 375g)
2 teaspoons baking powder
1 teaspoon salt
Flavouring (vanilla, almond extract, etc.—see step 3)

CUPCAKE TIP
The yogurt container will be your measuring cup – so no mess!

1. Preheat oven to 180°C/350°F/Gas Mark 4.

2. In a large bowl, mix the yogurt, sugar and eggs until completely blended with a whisk or a wooden spoon. Add oil and stir. Add flour, baking powder and salt and beat until smooth.

3. Add the flavouring of your choice – you could add 100g fresh, dried, or crystallized fruit or nuts. You can also add the flavouring extract of your choice – vanilla, almond, mint, lemon (with a little grated lemon rind), orange flower water, etc. Or you can add food colouring to make party or holiday cupcakes. Divide up the batter and make several different colours.

4. Spoon batter into cupcake papers, filling cups about ⅔ full. Cook cupcakes for about 25 minutes or until a tester inserted into the centre comes out clean. Remove from oven and cool.

VARIATION: FRUIT YOGURT CUPCAKES

Use the basic recipe above but instead of plain yogurt, use one with fruit or other ingredients already added.

★ If you are using a berry yogurt, add 100g dried, frozen or fresh fruit, cut into small pieces, or a tablespoon of kirsch or fruit liqueur.

★ If you are using apricot yogurt, add 2 tablespoons ground almonds and top the cooked cupcakes with apricot glaze and caramelized almonds.

★ If you are using strawberry or raspberry yogurt, top cooked cupcakes with whipped cream with added chopped fresh fruit.

POPPYSEED & LAVENDER HONEY Cupcakes

Cooking the poppyseeds in honey gives the cupcakes a distinctive flavour.

I prefer lavender honey but you can use the honey of your choice.

MAKES: ABOUT 24 REGULAR CUPCAKES OR 12 JUMBO CUPCAKES

200g poppyseeds
120ml honey
60ml water
375g plain flour
1 teaspoon bicarbonate of soda
1 teaspoon salt, plus a good pinch for
   egg whites
240g unsalted butter, room
   temperature
300g sugar
4 eggs, separated
1 teaspoon vanilla extract
240ml soured cream (you can use
   whipping or liquid cream instead)
Icing sugar for dusting

1. Preheat oven to 180°C/350°F/Gas Mark 4. Cook the poppyseeds with honey and water in a saucepan for about 5 minutes. Leave to cool.

2. Mix flour, bicarbonate of soda and salt together and set aside.

3. In the bowl of an electric mixer, cream butter with sugar until light and fluffy. Add cooled poppyseed mixture. Blend well. Add egg yolks, one at a time, beating well after each addition. Blend in vanilla and soured cream. Add dry ingredients to mixture, blending well.

4. Beat egg whites with a good pinch of salt until stiff but not dry. Gently fold into batter.

5. Spoon batter into either regular or jumbo cupcake papers, filling cups just a little over 1/2 full. Cook for about 15 minutes or until golden brown on top. Cooking time will depend on the size of the cupcakes you are making. Loosely cover cupcakes with a piece of aluminium foil and cook for another 5–10 minutes or until a tester comes out clean. Remove from oven and cool. Dust with icing sugar.

SUNSHINE & VITAMIN C
Cupcakes

Just what Grandma ordered! Besides being lovely to look at, these cupcakes provide a triple dose of vitamin C with the lemon, orange and grapefruit juices.

MAKES: ABOUT 16 CUPCAKES

300g plain flour

2 teaspoons baking powder

1 teaspoon salt

1 teaspoon each finely grated lemon, orange and grapefruit rind

125g unsalted butter, room temperature

250g sugar

2 eggs

160ml orange and grapefruit juice mixed (preferably in equal parts)

1 tablespoon lemon juice

THREE CITRUS FRUIT CUSTARD

3 tablespoons each of lemon juice, orange juice and grapefruit juice

80ml water

100g sugar

2 tablespoons plain flour

Pinch of salt

3 egg yolks (or 1 egg and 1 yolk)

Crystallized or jellied citrus fruit for decoration

1. Preheat oven to 180°C/350°F/Gas Mark 4.

2. Mix flour, baking powder and salt together in a medium bowl. Add the fruit rinds and set aside.

3. In the large bowl of an electric mixer, cream butter and sugar until light and fluffy. Add eggs, one at a time, mixing well after each addition. Alternately add dry ingredients and fruit juices, blending until smooth.

4. Fill cupcake papers about ⅔ full. Bake for about 25 minutes or until a tester inserted into the centre comes out clean. Remove from oven and cool.

5. Mix all the custard ingredients together in a large bowl over a saucepan of simmering water. Stir mixture constantly until it is hot to the touch and thick. It should coat the back of a wooden spoon.

6. Remove from heat and cool, stirring from time to time so that a skin doesn't form. When it has cooled, you can cover it with clingfilm and put it in the refrigerator until you are ready to use it. Heap onto cooled cupcakes and top with a piece of crystallized or jellied citrus fruit.

CUPCAKE TIP
You can also cut the centre out of the cupcakes and fill it with a portion of custard.

KIDS'
CUPCAKES

YETI Cupcakes

The Yeti, or the Abominable Snowman, is a mythical creature. The only thing that everyone agrees on about Yeti is that he is snow white — and very cool. Thus, the Yeti Cupcake!

MAKES: ABOUT 18 CUPCAKES

WHITE VELVET CUPCAKE
300g plain flour
2 teaspoons baking powder
1 teaspoon salt, plus a pinch for the
    egg whites
125g unsalted butter, room
    temperature
250g sugar
160ml milk
1 teaspoon vanilla extract (you can
    replace with another flavouring
    if you prefer: lemon, almond
    extract, etc.)
3 egg whites
115g mini-marshmallows

SNOW FROSTING
2 egg whites
150g sugar
60ml golden syrup
Pinch of salt
1 teaspoon vanilla extract
75g sweetened desiccated coconut
    (optional), plus extra for decoration

1. Preheat oven to 180°C/350°F/Gas Mark 4.

2. Mix flour, baking powder and salt together and set aside.

3. Cream butter and sugar until light and fluffy. Alternately add flour mixture and milk and beat until batter is smooth. Add flavouring.

4. Beat egg whites with a pinch of salt until stiff but not dry. Gently fold into batter. Fold in mini-marshmallows.

5. Spoon batter into cupcake papers, filling cups about ⅔ full. Bake for 20–25 minutes or until tester inserted into the centre comes out clean. Remove from oven and cool.

6. To make the frosting: in a large bowl mix egg whites, sugar, golden syrup and salt until combined. Place the bowl over simmering water and whisk until the sugar dissolves and the mixture is hot. This will take about 3 minutes. Remove from heat and beat for 5–7 minutes until frosting is cool and stiff peaks form. Beat in vanilla and delicately fold in the coconut by hand, if desired. The frosting will be ready to spread. Decorate frosted cupcakes to your taste.

CUPCAKE TIP
This is one version of what is know as a "7-minute frosting." It is light and delicious and has a marshmallow feel to it.

CHOCOLATE HAZELNUT

Cupcakes with Chocolate Hazelnut Spread

Chocolate hazelnut spreads are a great favourite among French children (and adults!) on a fresh baguette or a hot crêpe for breakfast or a snack. These light cupcakes will be a big success for any kid's birthday party or a special dessert for the whole family.

MAKES: ABOUT 16 CUPCAKES

250g plain flour
2 teaspoons baking powder
½ teaspoon salt
125g unsalted butter, room
   temperature
100g sugar
3 eggs
400g chocolate hazelnut spread
   (Nutella or similar)
60ml milk
65g roasted ground hazelnuts or
   whole hazelnuts for topping
   (optional)

1. Preheat oven to 180°C/350°F/Gas Mark 4.

2. Mix flour, baking powder and salt together and set aside.

3. Cream butter and sugar until light and fluffy. Add eggs, one at a time, mixing well after each addition. Add half of the chocolate hazelnut spread and blend thoroughly. Alternately add flour mixture and milk, blending well after each addition.

4. Spoon batter into cupcake papers, filling about ⅔ full. Bake for 20–25 minutes or until a tester inserted into the centre comes out clean. Remove from oven and cool.

5. When cupcakes are cool, generously ice them with remaining chocolate hazelnut spread. Sprinkle with roasted ground hazelnuts or place whole or half hazelnuts on top of each cupcake.

ROOT BEER Floats

Root beer floats were a staple of my childhood and teenage years and the mere thought brings back memories of hot summers where I grew up. My parents used to take us to the ice cream shop where we could indulge in what seemed at the time like a mile-high root beer float. Try one of these on a warm summer day and see if it has the same effect on you!

MAKES: ABOUT 16 CUPCAKES

150g plain flour
200g sugar
1 teaspoon baking powder
1 teaspoon bicarbonate of soda
1 teaspoon salt
120ml root beer
125g unsalted butter, cut into small
    pieces
1 egg, slightly beaten
80ml buttermilk
1 teaspoon vanilla extract
115g mini-marshmallows (optional)

ROOT BEER FROSTING

300g icing sugar
Pinch of salt
60ml root beer
125g unsalted butter, cut into small
    pieces
1 teaspoon vanilla extract
Whipped cream for topping
Root beer sweets (optional) for
    decoration
Decorative straws

1. Preheat oven to 180°C/350°F/Gas Mark 4.

2. In a large bowl, mix flour, sugar, baking powder, bicarbonate of soda and salt together and set aside.

3. In a heavy saucepan, bring root beer and butter to the boil, stirring constantly. Remove from heat and pour into flour mixture, beating well with a wooden spoon. Add egg, buttermilk and vanilla. When batter is smooth, fold in mini-marshmallows.

4. Spoon batter into cupcake papers, filling cups about ⅔ full. Bake for 20–25 minutes or until a tester inserted into the centre comes out clean. Remove from oven and cool.

5. To make the frosting: place icing sugar and salt in a large bowl.

6. In a heavy saucepan, bring root beer and butter to the boil, stirring constantly. Remove from heat and slowly add to sugar, stirring continually until mixture is smooth. When frosting has cooled, beat it for a few minutes with an electric beater. Frost cupcakes and top each cupcake with a dollop of whipped cream and a root beer sweet, if desired. Cut pretty straws in half and stick one into each cupcake.

BIRTHDAY Beauties

You can of course use any recipe for a birthday cake but I have suggested three here that are sure to please the kids – strawberry, lemon and chocolate. My mother used to make these for my birthday parties when I was little and ice them with lovely pastel-coloured frosting.

MAKES: ABOUT 12 CUPCAKES

STRAWBERRY CUPCAKE
375g plain flour
150g sugar
2½ teaspoons baking powder
1 teaspoon bicarbonate of soda
½ teaspoon salt
240ml buttermilk
185g unsalted butter, melted and
    slightly cooled
2 eggs, slightly beaten
1 teaspoon vanilla extract
175g fresh strawberries, cleaned and
    cut into small pieces

PASTEL CUPCAKE ICING
1 x quantity ready-to-use
    fondant icing (about 240ml per
    12 cupcakes)
Food colouring (various colours)

FOR DECORATION
Desiccated coconut
Chocolate sprinkles
Sweets
Coloured sugars
Crystallized fruits
Nuts

1. Preheat oven to 180°C/350°F/Gas Mark 4. In a large bowl, mix flour, sugar, baking powder, bicarbonate of soda and salt together and set aside.

2. In another bowl, mix buttermilk, melted butter, eggs and vanilla. Add liquid ingredients to dry ingredients and beat well with a wooden spoon. Fold in strawberries.

3. Spoon batter into cupcake papers, filling cups about ⅔ full. Bake for 20–25 minutes or until a tester inserted into the centre comes out clean. Remove from oven and cool.

4. To make the pastel icing: put fondant icing in separate bowls and add several drops of food colouring to each bowl until you obtain the desired colour. Ice or dip cupcakes in icing and decorate with desiccated coconut, chocolate sprinkles, sweets, coloured sugars, crystallized fruits, nuts, etc.

VARIATION: LEMON CUPCAKES

Follow recipe for Easter Lemon Chiffon Cupcakes (page 126) and top with the pastel cupcake icing. Decorate as desired.

VARIATION: CHOCOLATE CUPCAKES

Follow any of the chocolate cupcake recipes in this book, such as Chocolate Hazelnut Cupcake (page 44) or Chocolate Malted Milkshake Cupcake (page 58). Decorate as desired.

CHOCOLATE SUNDAE Cupcakes

These one-egg cupcakes will be light and velvety and the vanilla bean will give them an unrivalled flavour.

MAKES: ABOUT 18 CUPCAKES

REAL VANILLA CUPCAKE
180ml milk
1 vanilla pod, split lengthways
300g plain flour
2 teaspoons baking powder
1 teaspoon salt
125g unsalted butter, room
   temperature
200g sugar
1 egg

OLD-FASHIONED FUDGE FROSTING
300g sugar
180ml milk
2 tablespoons cocoa powder
Pinch of salt
1 tablespoon unsalted butter
1 teaspoon vanilla extract
60g finely ground peanuts (optional)
Maraschino cherries for decoration

1. In a small saucepan, heat milk with vanilla pod. When milk boils, remove from heat immediately and leave to cool, about an hour. After the milk has cooled, remove the vanilla pod and scrape out the seeds inside into the milk Discard the pod.

2. Preheat oven to 180°C/350°F/Gas Mark 4. Mix flour, baking powder and salt together and set aside.

3. Cream butter and sugar until light and fluffy. Add egg and beat well. Alternately add dry ingredients and milk, mixing well after each addition.

4. Spoon batter into cupcake papers, filling cups about ⅔ full. Bake for about 15–20 minutes or until a tester inserted into the centre comes out clean. Remove from oven and cool.

5. To make the frosting: mix sugar, milk, cocoa and salt in a medium saucepan. Cook slowly over medium heat until mixture comes to the boil. Continue cooking until mixture forms a soft ball when dropped into a glass of water (about 120°C/234°F on a sugar thermometer). This may take 15 minutes. Remove mixture from heat. Add butter and vanilla and blend well.

6. Put pan in cold water and beat until mixture is of spreading consistency. This could take 15 minutes. Spread on cupcakes immediately, sprinkle with peanuts, if desired, and top with a cherry before the frosting hardens.

COOKIES 'N' CREAM
Cupcakes

Remember when you were a kid and you used to dunk those cookies in a tall glass of cold milk? Well, this is the cupcake version. Use any type of sandwich cookie – choose your favourite.

MAKES: ABOUT 18–20 CUPCAKES

250g plain flour
2 teaspoons baking powder
1 teaspoon salt
125g unsalted butter, room
 temperature
200g sugar
2 eggs
1 teaspoon vanilla extract
180ml single cream
115g coarsely crushed sandwich
 cookies (e.g. Oreos)

WHITE CHOCOLATE
CREAM CHEESE FROSTING
180g good quality white chocolate,
 broken into pieces
180g cream cheese, softened, cut into
 pieces
185g unsalted butter, room
 temperature,
 cut into pieces
Miniature sandwich cookies or
 crushed cookies for decoration

1. Preheat oven to 180°C/350°F/Gas Mark 4.

2. Mix flour, baking powder and salt together and set aside.

3. Cream butter and sugar until light and fluffy. Add eggs, one at a time, mixing well after each addition. Add vanilla. Alternately add flour mixture and single cream and beat until batter is smooth. Fold in crushed cookies.

4. Spoon batter into cupcake papers, filling cups about ⅔ full. Bake for 20–25 minutes or until a tester inserted into the centre comes out clean. Remove from oven and cool.

5. To make the frosting: in a large bowl over simmering water melt white chocolate until smooth and creamy, just a few minutes. It should be just warm to the touch.

6. Beat the cream cheese and butter until light and fluffy. Add melted chocolate and beat again until smooth. Use the frosting immediately or it will harden. Press in a small cookie or sprinkle with crushed cookies at once, while frosting is still soft. This frosting looks like the cream filling in sandwich cookies.

HOT CHOCOLATE & MARSHMALLOW
Cupcakes

Serve these delicious chocolate cupcakes while they are still warm to get the full effect.

MAKES: ABOUT 12 CUPCAKES

240g dark chocolate
250g unsalted butter, room
   temperature
4 eggs
200g sugar
120g plain flour
1 teaspoon salt
60g mini-chocolate chips or grated
   chocolate
Marshmallows or mini-marshmallows
   for decoration

1. Preheat oven to 180°F/350°F/Gas mark 4. Melt chocolate and butter in a large bowl over a saucepan of simmering water until just melted (do not cook). Set aside until just warm.

2. Cream the eggs and sugar together until light and foamy. Add flour and salt and mix. Pour in the chocolate mixture and beat until batter is smooth.

3. Spoon batter into 12 cupcake papers. Sprinkle a teaspoon of mini-chocolate chips or grated chocolate over each cupcake and bake for 15 minutes. Remove cupcakes from oven. They will be very moist inside.

4. Place a marshmallow or several mini-marshmallows on each cupcake. Put cupcakes under grill for a few seconds until marshmallows start to brown. This will take only a second so be very careful. Remove from oven and wait for about 5 minutes before eating since the marshmallows will be very hot. These cupcakes are best eaten while still slightly warm.

CUPCAKE TIP
Alternatively, bake in a silicone mould. Leave off the marshmallow and sprinkle with a few grains of "fleur de sel."

JAM-FILLED Cupcakes

These cupcakes are perfect for any occasion and can be decorated accordingly for birthdays or holidays or for a special dessert or snack.

MAKES: **ABOUT 12 CUPCAKES**

BASIC YELLOW CUPCAKE
225g plain flour
2 teaspoons baking powder
1 teaspoon salt
125g unsalted butter, room
   temperature
200g sugar
2 eggs
1 teaspoon vanilla extract (or another
   flavouring, such as almond extract,
   orange flower water, etc.)
120ml milk
Jam, marmalade or preserves of
   your choice

BASIC WHITE CUPCAKE ICING
3 tablespoons hot milk or cream
375g icing sugar

FOR DECORATION
Coloured sugars
Sweets
Stencils etc.

1. Preheat oven to 180°C/350°F/Gas Mark 4. Mix dry ingredients together and set aside.

2. Cream butter and sugar until light and fluffy. Add eggs, one at a time, mixing well after each addition. Add vanilla. Alternately add flour mixture and milk and beat until batter is smooth.

3. Spoon batter into cupcake papers, filling cups about $^2/_3$ full. Bake for 20–25 minutes or until tester inserted into the centre comes out clean. Remove from oven and cool.

4. When cupcakes are cool, scoop out the centre and fill with the jam, marmalade or preserves of your choice. Replace the core.

5. Put hot milk or cream in a large bowl. Gradually add sugar until icing is thick enough to spread. Beat for several minutes until icing is smooth and creamy. You may need to add more sugar or liquid to get the right consistency but remember to beat well after each addition.

6. Ice the cooled cupcakes. While the icing is still soft, decorate with coloured sugars, sweets, stencils, etc.

VARIATION: BASIC CHOCOLATE CUPCAKE

Use the recipe for Basic Yellow Cupcake but replace 35g flour with 35g cocoa powder.

VARIATION: BASIC CHOCOLATE CUPCAKE ICING

Use the recipe for Basic White Cupcake Icing but replace 35g icing sugar with 35g cocoa powder.

PEANUT BUTTER & JAM SWIRLS

These cupcakes are definitely a throwback to childhood and those peanut butter and jam sandwiches of my youth.

MAKES: **ABOUT 20 CUPCAKES**

375g plain flour
3 teaspoons baking powder
1 teaspoon salt
125g unsalted butter, room temperature
300g soft light brown sugar
200g chunky peanut butter
1 teaspoon vanilla extract
3 eggs
240ml single cream
115g jam (about 6 heaped tablespoons)

PEANUT BUTTER FROSTING
60g unsalted butter, room temperature
125g smooth peanut butter
300g icing sugar
2 tablespoons milk

FOR DECORATION
65g chopped peanuts
Jam

1. Preheat oven to 180°C/350°F/Gas Mark 4.

2. Mix flour, baking powder and salt together and set aside.

3. Cream butter and sugar until light and fluffy. Add peanut butter and vanilla and continue beating until thoroughly blended. Add eggs, one at a time, mixing well after each addition. Alternately add single cream and dry ingredients, beating well after each addition.

4. Dollop the jam over the cupcake batter in 6 heaped tablespoons. Swirl jelly into batter with a long knife or spatula. Don't overmix.

5. Spoon batter into cupcake papers, filling cups about ⅔ full. Bake for 25–30 minutes or until a tester inserted in the centre comes out clean. Remove from oven and cool.

6. Make the frosting: cream butter, peanut butter and sugar together until light and fluffy. Gradually add milk and beat until creamy and of spreading consistency. You can add more milk if needed.

7. Frost cupcakes, add a swirl of jam and sprinkle with chopped peanuts.

CUPCAKE TIP
You can also fill the cupcake with jam rather than swirling it in – just take out the centre of a cooled cupcake with an apple corer, put a teaspoon of jam in the hole and replace the core.

ROCKY ROAD
Cupcakes

Rocky Road is a big favourite among kids. It is usually a combination of chocolate, walnuts, marshmallows and chocolate chips, whether it be in an ice cream, a brownie or a cupcake. You can improvize with this recipe – tailor it to your family and friends' tastes.

MAKES: ABOUT 18 CUPCAKES

225g plain flour
2 teaspoons baking powder
1 teaspoon salt
50g unsweetened cocoa powder
125g dark chocolate
60ml vegetable oil
1 egg
1 teaspoon vanilla extract
240ml milk
60g mini-marshmallows
60g dark chocolate chips,
    plus 60g for topping
60g coarsely chopped walnuts, plus
    60g for topping
60g white chocolate chips for topping
    (optional)

1. Preheat oven to 180°C/350°F/Gas Mark 4.

2. Mix flour, baking powder, salt and cocoa powder together, mix thoroughly, and set aside.

3. Melt chocolate in a bowl over a saucepan of simmering water (do not cook). Remove from heat as soon as chocolate is just melted. Using either an electric mixer or a wooden spoon, beat in oil, egg and vanilla. Alternately add flour mixture and milk, beating well after each addition. When batter is smooth and thoroughly blended, fold in 60g each mini-marshmallows, chocolate chips and walnuts.

4. Spoon batter into cupcake papers, filling just over ½ full. Mix remaining walnuts and chocolate chips together and sprinkle over batter. Bake for about 20 minutes or until topping is cooked. If the topping starts to burn before the cupcakes are cooked, cover lightly with a piece of aluminium foil. Remove from oven and cool.

CUPCAKE TIP
Try using different flavour chips (mint, peanut, coffee, etc.)

BANANA SPLIT
Cupcakes

Who doesn't remember banana splits from their childhood, when no one worried about their waistlines or cholesterol level!

MAKES: ABOUT 18 CUPCAKES

300g plain flour
2 teaspoons baking powder
1 teaspoon bicarbonate of soda
1 teaspoon salt
125g unsalted butter
300g sugar
2 eggs
1 teaspoon vanilla extract
2 ripe bananas, mashed
120ml buttermilk or soured cream
Strawberry preserves for filling

CHOCOLATE FUDGE ICING
65g unsalted butter, cut into little
    pieces
120g dark chocolate, broken
    into pieces
450g icing sugar
80ml hot milk
1 teaspoon vanilla extract
Pinch of salt
Maraschino cherries and banana
    sweets for decoration

1. Preheat oven to 180°C/350°F/Gas Mark 4.

2. Mix flour, baking powder, bicarbonate of soda and salt together and set aside.

3. Cream butter and sugar until light and fluffy. Add eggs, one at a time, mixing well after each addition. Add vanilla and mashed bananas and mix thoroughly. Alternately beat in flour mixture and liquid and blend until smooth.

4. Spoon batter into cupcake papers, filling cups about ⅔ full. Smooth batter with the back of a spoon. Bake for 20 minutes or until a tester inserted in the centre comes out clean. Remove from oven and cool.

5. When cupcakes are cool, scoop out the centre of each cupcake with an apple corer. Drop in a teaspoon of strawberry preserves.

6. To make the icing: melt butter and chocolate in a bowl over a saucepan of simmering water. Stir until just melted and set aside until cool to the touch. You can set the bowl in cold water to speed up the process.

7. Put sugar and hot milk in a large bowl and stir until smooth. Add vanilla, salt and chocolate mixture. Using an electric beater, beat icing until smooth and thickened, about 5 minutes. Ice cooled, filled cupcakes. Decorate with a cherry and banana sweets.

S'MORES Cupcakes

A S'more is a popular American sweet snack and consists of a sort of digestive biscuit sandwich with chocolate and marshmallows. Here is my cupcake version. I hope you will find it to your liking and will ask for s'more!

MAKES: ABOUT 18 CUPCAKES

DIGESTIVE BISCUIT AND MILK CHOCOLATE CUPCAKE
75g plain flour
175g finely crushed digestive biscuits (about 20 biscuits)
2 teaspoons baking powder
1 teaspoon salt
125g unsalted butter, room temperature
150g sugar
2 eggs
1 teaspoon vanilla extract
180ml milk
120g milk chocolate chips

NO-COOK MARSHMALLOW ICING
2 egg whites
Pinch of salt or 1/4 teaspoon cream of tartar
50g sugar
180ml golden syrup
Grated milk chocolate or chocolate sprinkles for decoration

1. Preheat oven to 180°C/350°F/Gas Mark 4.

2. Mix flour, crushed digestive biscuits, baking powder and salt together and set aside.

3. Cream butter and sugar until light and fluffy. Add eggs, one at a time, mixing well after each addition. Add vanilla. Alternately add flour mixture and milk and beat until batter is smooth. Fold in chocolate chips.

4. Spoon batter into cupcake papers, filling cups about ²⁄₃ full. Bake for 20–25 minutes or until a tester inserted into the centre comes out clean. Remove from oven and cool.

5. To make the icing: beat egg whites with salt or cream of tartar until soft peaks form. Gradually add sugar, beating continually. Slowly add golden syrup. Icing will form peaks and will have a marshmallow consistency. Ice cooled cupcakes and sprinkle with milk chocolate or chocolate sprinkles.

CUPCAKE TIP
For a cooked version of this icing, you can use the recipe for Snow Frosting, (page 42). You can also use ready-made marshmallow icing if you are in a hurry.

CHOCOLATE MALTED MILK SHAKE Cupcakes

These cupcakes remind me of those fabulous chocolate malted milk shakes we used to drink at the soda fountain of the local drug store when we were kids.

MAKES: **ABOUT 18 CUPCAKES**

150g chocolate malted milk sweets, crushed
75g chocolate malted milk powder
300g plain flour
3 teaspoons baking powder
1 teaspoon salt
375g unsalted butter, room temperature
200g soft light brown sugar
2 eggs
1 teaspoon vanilla extract
240ml single cream

CHOCOLATE MALTED MILK FROSTING

185g unsalted butter, room temperature
50g chocolate malted milk powder
300g icing sugar
Pinch of salt
60ml milk
1 teaspoon vanilla extract
Whipped cream (optional)
Chocolate malted milk sweets

1. Preheat oven to 180°C/350°F/Gas Mark 4.

2. In a small bowl, mix crushed chocolate malted milk sweets, malted milk powder, flour, baking powder and salt together. Set aside.

3. Cream butter and sugar until light and fluffy. Add eggs, one at a time, beating well after each addition. Add vanilla. Alternately add dry ingredients and single cream, beating until smooth after each addition.

4. Fill cupcake papers just a little over ½ full and bake for about 20 minutes or until a tester inserted into the centre comes out clean. Remove from oven and cool.

5. To make the frosting: beat butter, malted milk powder, sugar and salt until light and fluffy. Gradually add milk and vanilla, beating continuously, until frosting is of the desired consistency. You may want to use less milk. Frost cooled cupcakes, top with a dollop of whipped cream, if desired, and place a chocolate malted milk candy on top.

CUPCAKE TIP
Replace cream with low-fat milk for a lighter version.

AFTER DINNER
CUPCAKES

BURGUNDY BLUES
Cupcakes

Burgundy is one of the major wine-producing regions in France and some of the finest and best-known wines in the world are produced there. The combination of chocolate and red wine may seem strange at first but is actually quite delicious.

MAKES: ABOUT 16–18 CUPCAKES

110g plain flour
1 teaspoon baking powder
½ teaspoon salt
2 tablespoons cocoa powder
1 teaspoon cinnamon
125g unsalted butter, room
   temperature
100g sugar
2 eggs
60ml dry red wine
60g grated dark chocolate

CHOCOLATE GLAZE
125g good quality dark chocolate
60g unsalted butter
1 tablespoon golden syrup
Red and blue sugar for decoration

1. Preheat oven to 180°C/350°F/Gas Mark 4.

2. Mix dry ingredients together and set aside.

3. Cream butter and sugar until light and fluffy. Add eggs, one at a time, mixing well after each addition. Alternately beat in flour mixture and wine. Fold in grated chocolate.

4. Spoon batter into cupcake papers, filling cups about ⅔ full. Bake for 20–25 minutes or until a tester inserted into the centre comes out clean. Remove from oven and cool.

5. To make the chocolate glaze: melt chocolate and butter in a bowl over a saucepan of simmering water. When just melted and barely warm to the touch, remove from heat and stir in golden syrup. Either dip cooled cupcakes in glaze or dribble a little over each cupcake. Sprinkle with red and blue sugar.

CUPCAKE TIP
These cupcakes will go down particularly well with a glass of port wine or a cream sherry.

RUM RAISIN Cupcakes with Butter Rum Frosting

Rum and raisins are a very popular duo, and justifiably so. I think that the rum brings out the flavour of the raisins and vice versa. Make these in mini-cupcake moulds and serve them with rum and raisin ice cream for a special dessert treat.

MAKES: ABOUT 16 REGULAR CUPCAKES OR 40 MINI-CUPCAKES

100g raisins
60ml dark rum
185g plain flour
1½ teaspoons baking powder
1 teaspoon salt
150g unsalted butter, cut into small pieces
150g soft light brown sugar
3 eggs, slightly beaten

BUTTER RUM FROSTING
60g unsalted butter, room temperature
300g icing sugar
Pinch of salt
3 tablespoons rum (use raisin-soaking liquid)
Raisins for decoration

1. Soak raisins in rum for about 30 minutes, turning from time to time. Drain and set aside. Save liquid for frosting.

2. Preheat oven to 180°C/350°F/Gas Mark 4.

3. In a large bowl, mix flour, baking powder and salt together and set aside.

4. In a small saucepan, melt butter and sugar over low heat, stirring constantly. When sugar has dissolved, remove from heat and pour into the centre of the flour mixture. Mix well. Add drained raisins and eggs and stir vigorously with a wooden spoon until the batter is smooth.

5. Fill cupcake papers about ⅔ full. Bake for about 25 minutes or until a tester inserted into the centre comes out clean. Remove from oven and cool.

6. To make the frosting: cream butter, sugar and salt until light and fluffy. Add rum and continue beating. If too thick, add more rum; if too thin, add more sugar. Frost cooled cupcakes and decorate with raisins.

BEER & PEANUTS
Cupcakes

These original and spectacular looking cupcakes will almost make you feel like you are sitting in a cosy pub in merry old England, downing a pint of ale and munching on some peanuts.

MAKES: ABOUT 12–14 CUPCAKES

240ml dark beer
130g soft light brown sugar
90g unsalted butter, cut into pieces
100g raisins
250g plain flour
2 teaspoons baking powder
1 teaspoon bicarbonate of soda
1 teaspoon salt
1 teaspoon cinnamon
½ teaspoon ground ginger
Dash of grated nutmeg
2 eggs, slightly beaten

PEANUT BRITTLE TOPPING
90g unsalted butter
100g soft light brown sugar
2 tablespoons sugar syrup (ready-made or boil equal amounts of sugar and water)
½ teaspoon lemon juice
200g grilled peanuts, lightly salted

1. In a large saucepan, bring beer, sugar and butter to the boil. Add raisins and cook for 5 minutes over medium heat. Remove from heat and let cool, stirring from time to time so that a crust doesn't form.

2. Preheat oven to 180°C/350°F/Gas Mark 4.

3. In a large bowl, mix dry ingredients together. Pour in cooled beer mixture and blend well. Add eggs, a little at a time, and continue mixing until batter is smooth.

4. Spoon batter into cupcake papers, filling cups about ½ full. Bake for about 15–20 minutes or until just starting to brown on top. Remember, they are going to cook for another 5–7 minutes.

5. While the cupcakes are cooking, make the topping. In a heavy saucepan, mix butter, sugar, syrup and lemon juice and heat slowly until all of the sugar has dissolved, stirring from time to time. Continue to cook over a low heat for another 5 minutes. Stir in peanuts and cook for a further 2 minutes.

6. Spread a layer of peanut topping over each cupcake. Return to oven and cook for 5–7 minutes. When peanuts start to brown, remove from oven and leave to cool in pan before removing cupcakes.

KIR Cupcakes

The inspiration for these cupcakes is the 'Kir,' a cocktail made with white wine and blackcurrant liqueur (Crème de Cassis). It originated in Dijon but is found in bars and on tables throughout France.

MAKES: ABOUT 20 CUPCAKES

250g plain flour
250g sugar
2 teaspoons baking powder
½ teaspoon salt, plus pinch for the egg whites
120ml vegetable oil
120ml white wine
4 eggs, separated
150g dried currants

BLACKCURRANT GLAZE
150g blackcurrant jam (about 8 heaped tablespoons)
2 tablespoons blackcurrant liqueur (optional)

FOR DECORATION
White decorator icing
Red or black currants (optional)

1. Preheat oven to 180°C/350°F/Gas Mark 4.

2. Mix flour, sugar, baking powder and salt in a bowl. Gradually add liquid, mixing well. Add egg yolks, beating well after each addition. The batter should be smooth and light.

3. Beat egg whites with a pinch of salt until stiff but not dry. Gently fold into batter. Carefully fold in dried currants.

4. Fill cupcake papers about ¾ full with the mixture and bake for about 20 minutes or until a tester inserted into the centre comes out clean. Remove from oven and cool.

5. To make the glaze: In a small saucepan, heat blackcurrant jam with liqueur, if using, and cook for about 2 minutes. With a pastry brush, spread glaze on cooled cupcakes.

6. When glaze has cooled, decorate with a zigzag of white decorator icing and fresh currants (red or black) if the season permits.

CUPCAKE TIP
If you want to make a 'Kir Royale,' replace the white wine in the cupcake batter with champagne.

CAPPUCCINO Cupcakes

This light coffee cupcake with its meringue-like cooked coffee frosting is a delight to the eyes and a wonderful accompaniment to a real cappuccino at any time of the day.

MAKES: ABOUT 12 CUPCAKES

150g plain flour
2 teaspoons baking powder
1 teaspoon salt
375g unsalted butter, room temperature
150g soft light brown sugar
2 eggs
1 tablespoon coffee extract
120ml single cream

STEAMED COFFEE FROSTING
250g soft light brown sugar
3 tablespoons extra-strong coffee
2 egg whites
$\frac{1}{4}$ teaspoon baking powder or cream of tartar
Cocoa powder or cinnamon for dusting
Chocolate sprinkles or chocolate coffee beans (optional) for decoration

1. Preheat oven to 180°C/350°F/Gas Mark 4.

2. Sift flour, baking powder and salt together and set aside.

3. Cream butter and sugar until light and fluffy. Add eggs, one at a time, blending well after each addition. Add coffee extract. Alternately add dry ingredients and single cream, beating until smooth.

4. Divide batter between 12 cupcake papers. Cook for 25 minutes or until a tester inserted into the centre comes out clean. Remove from oven and cool.

5. To make the frosting: mix all ingredients in a large bowl. Place the bowl over rapidly boiling water and beat for about 7 minutes with an electric or rotary beater until frosting stands in peaks.

6. Remove from heat and spread on cupcakes or apply a generous spoonful to each cupcake. Sprinkle with cocoa powder before frosting hardens. Frosting will be hard on the outside and creamy on the inside. Sprinkle with chocolate sprinkles and put a chocolate coffee bean on top, if using. This is another variation on a 7-minute frosting.

CUBA LIBRE
Cupcakes

A 'Cuba Libre' (Free Cuba) is generally a cocktail made with rum and cola and served with a lime wedge. Its origins are widely disputed but let's hope that its metamorphosis into a cupcake will meet with widespread approval!

MAKES: ABOUT 12 CUPCAKES

125g unsalted butter, cut into small
    pieces
120ml cola
150g plain flour
1 teaspoon baking powder
1 teaspoon bicarbonate of soda
$\frac{1}{2}$ teaspoon salt
200g sugar
60ml buttermilk
1 egg, slightly beaten
1 teaspoon vanilla extract

RUM FROSTING
125g unsalted butter, room
    temperature
300g icing sugar
Pinch of salt
2 tablespoons dark rum
Crystallized or jellied lime slices for
    decoration

1. In a medium saucepan, heat butter and cola until it boils. Remove from heat and leave to cool, about 10–15 minutes (you can set it in a pan of cold water to speed up the process).

2. Preheat oven to 180°C/350°F/Gas Mark 4.

3. In a large mixing bowl, combine flour, baking powder, bicarbonate of soda, salt and sugar. Add cooled liquid to mixture and stir vigorously until batter is smooth and well blended. Beat in buttermilk, egg and vanilla.

4. Spoon batter into cupcake papers, filling cups about $\frac{2}{3}$ full. Bake for 20–25 minutes or until a tester inserted into the centre comes out clean. Remove from oven and cool.

5. To make the frosting: cream butter, sugar and salt until light and fluffy. Gradually add rum, beating continually until frosting is of spreading consistency. Frost cooled cupcakes. Decorate with crystallized or jellied lime slices.

IRISH COFFEE
Cupcakes

These cupcakes are a bit reminiscent of Irish soda bread, but with a dose of whiskey for good measure. The Mocha Butter Cream Frosting adds an elegant touch.

MAKES: ABOUT 16 CUPCAKES

225g plain flour
150g soft light brown sugar
1 teaspoon baking powder
1 teaspoon bicarbonate of soda
1 teaspoon salt
1 teaspoon cinnamon
½ teaspoon ground ginger
Dash of grated nutmeg
100g dark raisins
65g coarsely chopped nuts
   (pistachios, walnuts, or hazelnuts)
2 eggs, slightly beaten
120ml vegetable oil
120ml Irish whiskey
60ml single cream or milk

MOCHA BUTTER CREAM FROSTING

250g unsalted butter, room
   temperature, cut into small pieces
250g icing sugar
2 egg yolks
1 tablespoon coffee extract or very
   strong coffee (more or less,
   depending on your taste)

1. Preheat oven to 180°C/350°F/Gas Mark 4.

2. In a large bowl, mix all of the dry ingredients together. Add eggs, oil, whiskey and cream or milk to dry ingredients and mix until thoroughly blended with a wooden spoon.

3. Fill cupcake papers about ⅔ full. Bake for 25–30 minutes or until a tester inserted into the centre comes out clean. Remove from oven and cool.

4. To make the frosting: cream butter and sugar together until light and fluffy. Add egg yolks and coffee extract to taste and beat until mixture is light, shiny and of good spreading consistency (at least 10 minutes). Frost cooled cupcakes.

CUPCAKE TIP
If you don't have the time or are otherwise inclined, frost these cupcakes with coffee-flavoured whipped cream or use the Irish Whiskey Frosting (page 124).

MINT JULEP
Cupcakes

A mint julep is a cocktail composed of fresh mint, bourbon and crushed ice. It is traditionally served in an iced pewter or silver mug during the Kentucky Derby in America.

MAKES: ABOUT 18 CUPCAKES

150g plain flour
1 teaspoon baking powder
1 teaspoon salt
185g unsalted butter, room temperature
200g sugar
3 eggs
120ml bourbon
15g fresh finely chopped mint

WHITE CHOCOLATE MINT FROSTING
120ml whipping cream
1 tablespoon unsalted butter
240g white chocolate
2 tablespoons crème de menthe (or any other mint liqueur)
Green food colouring (optional)

FOR DECORATION
Several sprigs of fresh mint
Green sugar (optional)
Decorative straws

1. Preheat oven to 180°C/350°F/Gas Mark 4.

2. Mix flour, baking powder and salt together and set aside.

3. Cream butter and sugar until light and fluffy. Add eggs, one at a time, mixing well after each addition. Alternately beat in flour mixture and bourbon. Fold in fresh mint.

4. Spoon batter into cupcake papers, filling cups about ⅔ full. Bake for 20–25 minutes or until a tester inserted into the centre comes out clean. Remove from oven and cool.

5. To make the frosting: heat cream and butter in a saucepan over medium heat, stirring until butter melts. Remove from heat and add white chocolate. Stir until melted. Add mint liqueur and food colouring, if desired. Transfer frosting to a bowl and leave to cool, stirring from time to time, until it is of spreading consistency. This will probably take about 2 hours. You can speed up the process by putting the bowl in cold water.

6. Frost cooled cupcakes and decorate with a sprig of mint. Alternatively, you can dip the cupcakes in the frosting once the mixture has cooled a bit. Decorate immediately with green sugar and a mint sprig before frosting hardens. Stick in a little straw for good measure.

MEZZO-MEZZO Cupcakes

Chocolate and coffee are an irresistible duo. These soured cream cupcakes will be a gourmet ending to any gourmet meal.

MAKES: ABOUT 16 REGULAR CUPCAKES, 8 JUMBO CUPCAKES OR 40 MINI-CUPCAKES

200g plain flour
2 teaspoons baking powder
1 teaspoon bicarbonate of soda
1 teaspoon salt
75g cocoa powder
200g soft light brown sugar
3 tablespoons instant cappuccino powder (you can use espresso or even decaffeinated coffee powder)
125g unsalted butter, melted and cooled
2 eggs, slightly beaten
240ml soured cream

CHOCOLATE WHIPPED CREAM FROSTING
240ml whipping cream, chilled
3 tablespoons sugar
1 tablespoon cocoa powder, plus more for dusting
1 tablespoon instant cappuccino powder (you can use espresso or decaffeinated coffee powder)
Chocolate coffee beans for decoration

1. Preheat oven to 180°C/350°F/Gas Mark 4.

2. In a large bowl, mix all of the dry ingredients together and set aside.

3. In another bowl, mix butter, eggs and soured cream together. Pour into dry ingredients, rapidly mixing with a wooden spoon until batter is smooth.

4. Spoon batter into cupcake papers, filling cups about $2/3$ full. Cook for 15–20 minutes or until a tester inserted into the centre comes out clean. Remove from oven and cool.

5. To make the frosting: put cream, sugar, cocoa and coffee powder in a large bowl. Stir, cover and leave in the refrigerator for about an hour, until chocolate and coffee have dissolved. Remove from refrigerator and beat with an electric beater until stiff.

6. Frost cooled cupcakes just before serving. Dust with cocoa powder and top each cupcake with a chocolate coffee bean.

CUPCAKE TIP
Serve with a little cup of espresso on the side.

MARGARITA
Cupcakes with Lime Glaze

For this cupcake version of a margarita cocktail, I have recommended using coarse sugar to imitate the salt but if you are particularly daring you could put a few grains of 'fleur de sel' on top. The contrast of the very sweet lime glaze and the salt would certainly take one back to this cupcake's origins.

MAKES: ABOUT 18 CUPCAKES

150g plain flour
1 teaspoon baking powder
½ teaspoon salt, plus pinch for the egg whites
125g unsalted butter, room temperature
150g sugar
3 eggs, separated
1 tablespoon finely grated lime rind
2 tablespoons tequila

LIME GLAZE
2 tablespoons fresh lime juice
150g icing sugar
1 tablespoon tequila
Green food colouring (optional)
Coarse sugar (or salt, see step 6)
Lime slices for decoration

1. Preheat oven to 180°C/350°F/Gas Mark 4.

2. Mix flour, baking powder and salt together and set aside.

3. Cream butter and sugar until light and fluffy. Add egg yolks, one at a time, mixing well after each addition. Add lime rind and tequila. Gradually stir in dry ingredients until all of the flour is absorbed and the batter is smooth.

4. Beat egg whites with a pinch of salt until stiff but not dry. Gently fold whites into batter.

5. Fill cupcake papers a little over ½ full. Bake for about 20–25 minutes or until a tester inserted into the centre comes out clean. Remove from oven and cool.

6. To make the glaze: in a medium bowl, mix the lime juice, icing sugar and tequila and beat until smooth and blended. Stir in green food colouring, if desired. Brush cooled cupcakes with glaze and sprinkle with coarse sugar (or a few grains of 'fleur de sel'). Decorate with a lime slice.

MIDNIGHT MADNESS Cupcakes

Wait until midnight and surprise your guests with these indulgent little black gems.

MAKES: ABOUT 20 CUPCAKES

185g plain flour
150g soft light brown sugar
35g cocoa powder
2 teaspoons baking powder
½ teaspoon salt
180ml water
60ml vegetable oil
1 egg, lightly beaten
1 teaspoon vanilla extract

FILLING
240g cream cheese
65g sugar
1 egg
½ teaspoon salt
1 tablespoon rum or brandy (optional)
120g chocolate chips

MIDNIGHT SKY FROSTING
375g sugar
2 egg whites
Pinch of salt or cream of tartar
Black food colouring

FOR DECORATION
Glitter sugar for dusting
Silver balls and banana shaped sweets

1. Preheat oven to 180°C/350°F/Gas Mark 4.

2. To make the filling: beat cream cheese, sugar, egg, salt and rum until smooth. Fold in chocolate chips and set aside.

3. Mix flour, sugar, cocoa powder, baking powder and salt in a large bowl. Add water, oil, egg and vanilla and beat with a wooden spoon until smooth.

4. Fill cupcake papers ½ full with chocolate batter. Place a heaped teaspoon of the cream cheese mixture on each. Bake for about 15–25 minutes or until firm to the touch. The cream cheese filling will be a bit soft. Remove from oven and cool.

5. To make the frosting: using an electric beater, beat sugar with egg whites and salt or cream of tartar until mixed. Increase speed to high and beat for about 5 minutes or until very thick and fluffy. Add black food colouring. Frost cooled cupcakes and dust with glitter sugar, silver balls and banana shaped sweets for the moon.

CUPCAKE TIP
Alternatively, instead of making Midnight Sky Frosting you could top with ready-to-use black cake icing.

PINA COLADA
Cupcakes

The main ingredients in a Piña Colada cocktail, just like in this cupcake, are pineapple, coconut and rum. Sit back, enjoy and listen to the palm trees swaying in the ocean breeze.

MAKES: **ABOUT 16–18 CUPCAKES**

300g plain flour
2 teaspoons baking powder
1 teaspoon salt, plus pinch for the
   egg whites
125g unsalted butter, room
   temperature
250g sugar
2 eggs, separated
120ml pineapple juice
60ml light rum (or coconut cream or
   more pineapple juice)
75g desiccated coconut

COCONUT ICING
2 egg whites
Pinch of salt
300g icing sugar
75g desiccated coconut

FOR DECORATION
Toasted desiccated coconut
Dried or crystallized pineapple

1. Preheat oven to 180°C/350°F/Gas Mark 4.

2. Mix together flour, baking powder and salt together in a bowl and set aside.

3. Cream butter and sugar until light and fluffy. Add egg yolks, one at a time, mixing well after each addition. Alternately beat in flour mixture and liquid and blend until smooth. Stir in coconut. Beat egg whites with pinch of salt until stiff but not dry and gently fold into mixture.

4. Spoon batter into cupcake papers, filling cups about ⅔ full, smoothing with the back of a spoon. Bake for 20–25 minutes or until a tester inserted into the centre comes out clean. Remove from oven and cool.

5. To make the icing: beat egg whites with a pinch of salt until stiff but not dry. Add sugar by heaped tablespoons, beating continually. Fold in dessicated coconut. Add additional icing sugar if necessary so that icing holds its shape. Ice cooled cupcakes and sprinkle with toasted coconut and a piece of dried or crystallized pineapple.

PASTIS Cupcakes with Anise Frosting

'Pastis' is an anise-based liqueur, diluted with water, and extremely popular in the south of France as an aperitif. Any brand will do. The result is surprising and extraordinary – a delicate anise-flavoured batter, topped with creamy anise-flavoured butter cream frosting.

MAKES: ABOUT 18 CUPCAKES

200g plain flour
2 teaspoons baking powder
1 teaspoon salt
180g unsalted butter, room
  temperature
150g sugar
3 eggs
60ml pastis

ANISE BUTTER CREAM FROSTING
240g unsalted butter, room
  temperature, cut into small pieces
250g icing sugar
Pinch of salt
2 tablespoons pastis (or anise syrup
  or liquorice essence to taste)
Liquorice strands, liquorice sweets or
  black decorator icing for decoration

1. Preheat oven to 180°C/350°F/Gas Mark 4.

2. Mix flour, baking powder and salt together and set aside.

3. Cream butter and sugar until light and fluffy. Add eggs, one at a time, mixing well after each addition. Alternately beat in flour mixture and pastis.

4. Spoon batter into cupcake papers, filling cups about ⅔ full. Bake for 25 minutes or until a tester inserted into the centre comes out clean. Remove from oven and cool.

5. To make the frosting: in the large bowl of an electric mixer, beat butter, sugar and salt until light and fluffy. Add pastis and continue beating until of good spreading consistency. Frost cooled cupcakes. Decorate with a strand of liquorice (arranged in a spiral shape over the icing), liquorice sweets or black decorator icing.

CUPCAKE TIP
If you prefer, use anise syrup for a non-alcoholic version.

AFTER EIGHT Cupcakes

These cupcakes will dazzle the eyes as well as the taste buds. When you bite into them — crispy on the outside and creamy on the inside — chocolate mint heaven, beyond a doubt!

MAKES: ABOUT 12 CUPCAKES

200g plain flour
50g cocoa powder
2 teaspoons baking powder
1 teaspoon salt
90g unsalted butter, room
    temperature
100g sugar
2 eggs
160ml single cream
Few drops of mint extract
60g miniature chocolate mint chips

MINT BUTTER CREAM FROSTING
185g unsalted butter, room
    temperature, cut into small pieces
300g icing sugar
2 tablespoons milk
Few drops of mint extract
Food colouring (optional)

CHOCOLATE GANACHE
150g dark chocolate, broken into
    little pieces
150ml double cream
12 little chocolate-covered mint
    patties (optional) for decoration

1. Preheat oven to 180°C/350°F/Gas Mark 4.

2. Mix flour, cocoa, baking powder and salt together and set aside.

3. Cream butter and sugar until light and fluffy. Add eggs, one at a time, mixing after each addition. Alternately beat in flour mixture and single cream. Add a few drops of mint extract to batter and mix well.

4. Spoon batter into 12 cupcake papers. Sprinkle chocolate mint chips over cupcakes and bake for 20–25 minutes or until a tester inserted into the centre comes out clean. Remove from oven and cool.

5. To make the frosting: cream butter and sugar until light and fluffy. Add milk and mint extract and mix well. You may want to add more or less milk. Add food colouring if you are using it. Spread over cooled cupcakes and set in a cool place until frosting has hardened.

6. To make the ganache: place chocolate and cream in a bowl over a saucepan of simmering water and heat until cream is warm to the touch and the chocolate starts to melt. Remove from heat and stir until all of the chocolate has melted and the mixture is homogeneous. Remember — you don't want to cook the chocolate, you just want to melt it. You can always put it back over the warm water for a few seconds if you need to. Cool slightly and dip cupcakes in chocolate ganache, leaving a little of the butter cream showing around the edges. Place a little chocolate-covered mint patty on top, if desired.

GOURMET
CUPCAKES

TARTE TATIN Cupcakes with Caramelized Apples

A Tarte Tatin is a French upside-down apple tart, one of the simplest and most delicious of traditional French desserts and very popular in my family, especially in the autumn when the apples are at their finest. This is my cupcake version.

MAKES: ABOUT 16 CUPCAKES

250g plain flour
2 teaspoons baking powder
1 teaspoon salt
100g soft light brown sugar
125g unsalted butter, room
    temperature
2 eggs, slightly beaten
120ml milk
1 teaspoon vanilla extract

CARAMELIZED APPLES

65g unsalted butter
4 apples, peeled, cored and cut into
    16 (cut each quarter into four
    parts, lengthwise)
4 tablespoons sugar

CARAMEL GLAZE

65g butter
50g soft light brown sugar
225g icing sugar
1 teaspoon vanilla extract
1 tablespoon milk

1. Preheat oven to 180°C/350°F/Gas Mark 4.

2. In a large bowl, mix flour, baking powder, salt and sugar. Add remaining cupcake ingredients and beat with a wooden spoon or whisk for 3 minutes.

3. Spoon batter into cupcake papers, filling about $^2/_3$ full. Bake for about 20 minutes or until a tester inserted into the centre comes out clean. Remove from oven and cool.

4. To caramelize the apples: in a large pan, melt the butter and lay out the pieces of apple, cooking them on both sides. When they are golden, sprinkle them with sugar and remove from heat. Arrange them attractively on the cupcakes, four apple sections per cupcake. You may want to cook the apples in two batches.

5. To make the glaze (or use ready-made caramel if you prefer): melt butter in a heavy saucepan over low heat. Add brown sugar and stir for about 3 minutes until sugar is melted. Remove from heat. Add icing sugar, vanilla and milk and blend with a whisk. Dribble about a tablespoon of caramel over each cupcake.

BOURDALOUE Cupcakes with Caramelized Almonds

Any preparation with the adjective 'Bourdaloue' attached to it means that it is prepared with some combination of pears and almonds. A cupcake 'à la Bourdaloue' – you guessed it – has pears and almonds as its main ingredients! These cupcakes are made in jumbo cupcake moulds and are not only delicious but are impressive to behold.

MAKES: **ABOUT 6–8 JUMBO CUPCAKES**

185g unsalted butter, room temperature
100g sugar
3 eggs
2 teaspoons vanilla extract
185g ground almonds
35g plain flour
1 teaspoon salt
6–8 pear halves, (fresh or canned), cut lengthways into quarters

CARAMELIZED ALMONDS
100g slivered almonds
50g sugar

1. Preheat oven to 180°C/350°F/Gas Mark 4.

2. Cream butter and sugar together until light and fluffy. Add eggs, one at a time, blending well after each addition. Add vanilla. Add ground almonds, flour and salt and mix until batter is smooth.

3. Divide batter between 6–8 jumbo cupcake papers. Place pear quarters in the centre, pressing in just slightly. Cook for 30 minutes or until cupcakes are golden brown and spring back to the touch. Remove from oven and cool before unmoulding.

4. Mix almonds and sugar in a cold non-stick pan. Turn heat to high, stirring constantly. When almonds start to brown (this will take only a few minutes), pour them immediately into a heat-proof dish. When they are completely cool, gently break them loose with a fork or your fingers. Sprinkle them over cupcakes just before serving.

CUPCAKE TIP
Bake these in a silicone mould and serve with custard sauce (see page 164)

CEVENOL Cupcakes with Crème de Marron icing

The Cevennes mountains in the south of France are known for their rustic landscapes and the chestnut trees that grow on their gentle slopes. Robert Louis Stevenson immortalized the Cevennes in a book that he wrote about a trip he took through these mountains with a donkey. The area is also known for its many local specialities made from chestnuts.

MAKES: ABOUT 16 CUPCAKES

100g plain flour
2 teaspoons baking powder
1 teaspoon salt
80g unsalted butter
400g 'crème de marron' chestnut spread (can be found in most gourmet food stores)
100g sugar
2 eggs
2 tablespoons rum
8 glazed chestnuts (can be found in most gourmet food stores) for decoration

1. Preheat oven to 180°C/350°F/Gas Mark 4.

2. Mix flour, baking powder and salt together and set aside.

3. In the large bowl of an electric mixer, cream butter and 200g chestnut spread until smooth and creamy. Add sugar, eggs and rum and beat until thoroughly blended. Mix in dry ingredients.

4. Spoon batter into cupcake papers, filling about $^2/_3$ full. Bake for about 25 minutes or until a tester inserted into the centre comes out clean. Remove from oven and cool.

5. Ice cooled cupcakes with remaining chestnut spread and top each cupcake with half a glazed chestnut.

CRÊPE SUZETTE CUPCAKES

A 'Crêpe Suzette' is a crêpe that is filled with a butter cream made with orange liqueur (Grand Marnier, Cointreau, Triple Sec, Curaçao, etc.) and flambéed before being eaten. This is the cupcake version, frosted with the same cream I use for my Crêpes Suzettes.

MAKES: **ABOUT 12 CUPCAKES**

300g plain flour
2 teaspoons baking powder
1 teaspoon salt
125g unsalted butter, room
    temperature
150g sugar
2 eggs
Juice and finely grated rind of
    1 medium-sized orange
2 tablespoons orange liqueur (Grand
    Marnier, Cointreau, Triple Sec,
    Curaçao, etc.)
Water, if necessary

SUZETTE FROSTING
160g unsalted butter, room
    temperature
150g sugar
Juice and finely grated rind of
    1 medium orange or two small
    tangerines
60ml orange liqueur
Crystallized orange peel for
    decoration

1. Preheat oven to 180°C/350°F/Gas Mark 4.

2. Mix flour, baking powder and salt together. Set aside.

3. Cream butter and sugar until light and fluffy. Add eggs, one at a time, beating thoroughly after each addition. Add orange rind. Combine orange juice and orange liqueur and add water, if necessary, to make 120ml. Alternately add dry ingredients and liquid to butter mixture, blending until batter is smooth.

4. Fill cupcake papers about ⅔ full and bake for about 20–25 minutes or until a tester inserted into the centre comes out clean. Remove from oven and cool.

5. To make the frosting: cream butter with sugar until it is light and fluffy. Slowly add the juice and rind of the orange or tangerines, beating continually. Carefully add the liqueur, little by little, making sure that the mixture doesn't curdle. Keep beating until mixture is of spreading consistency. Frost cooled cupcakes and decorate with a piece of crystallized orange peel. The butter will harden when it sets so make sure to frost the cupcakes while the frosting is still creamy.

CUPCAKE TIP
Suzette frosting is a challenge. You can replace it with any other orange frosting (see page 137)

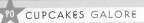

CHOCOLATE MOUSSE Cupcakes

The chocolate mousse cake that inspired this recipe was and still is my son's preferred birthday cake recipe. This 2-in-1 recipe includes both the batter and the frosting for these light and very moist cupcakes. For chocoholics only!

MAKES: ABOUT 12 CUPCAKES

4 heaped tablespoons plain flour
2½ teaspoons baking powder
½ teaspoon salt, plus good pinch for the egg whites
300g dark chocolate
250g unsalted butter, room temperature
6 eggs, separated
200g sugar
Grated chocolate for decoration

CUPCAKE TIP
You might want to double this recipe – you will never have too many.

1. Preheat oven to 180°C/350°F/Gas Mark 4.

2. Mix flour, baking powder and salt together and set aside.

3. Melt the chocolate and butter in a bowl over a pan of simmering water, or in a microwave. Don't cook – the chocolate and butter should be just melted. Stir and set aside.

4. Beat egg yolks and sugar until light yellow and foamy. Beat in the melted chocolate until totally blended.

5. Beat egg whites with a pinch of salt until stiff but not dry. Gently fold into chocolate mixture. Divide mixture into two parts and put one of them in the refrigerator to be used later to frost cupcakes. Gently whisk flour mixture into other half until it is completely absorbed.

6. Fill cupcake papers about ⅔ full with batter and bake for 15–20 minutes. Don't overcook. Cupcakes should be just cooked and moist in the centre. Remove from oven and cool.

7. When cupcakes are cool, frost with remaining chocolate mousse. Decorate with grated chocolate.

EARL GREY Cupcakes

The distinctive taste of Earl Grey tea is due to bergamot, a small tree in the orange family. The rind of the bergamot orange yields an aromatic oil, used in the tea and perfume industries.

MAKES: ABOUT 12 CUPCAKES

160ml whole milk
2 teaspoons loose or 2 tea bags
  Earl Grey tea
250g plain flour
2 teaspoons baking powder
1 teaspoon salt
125g unsalted butter, room
  temperature
200g sugar
2 eggs
3 tablespoons crystallized orange
  rind, chopped into little pieces
  (optional)

CHOCOLATE EARL GREY GANACHE
180g good quality dark chocolate,
  broken into pieces
20g unsalted butter, room
  temperature
120ml double cream
2 teaspoons loose or 2 tea bags
  Earl Grey tea

1. In a small saucepan, heat milk with tea. Bring to the boil and then remove from heat and let steep until milk is cool to the touch, about 30 minutes. Filter the tea or remove tea bags and set liquid aside.

2. Preheat oven to 180°C/350°F/Gas Mark 4.

3. Mix flour, baking powder and salt together and set aside.

4. Cream butter and sugar together until light and fluffy. Add eggs, one at a time, mixing well after each addition. Alternately beat in dry ingredients and liquid. Fold in crystallized orange rind, if desired.

5. Spoon batter into cupcake papers, filling cups about $2/3$ full. Bake for about 25 minutes or until a tester inserted into the centre comes out clean. Remove from oven and cool.

6. To make the ganache: put chocolate and butter in a large mixing bowl and set aside. Combine cream and tea in a small pan and slowly bring to the boil. Remove from heat, cover and let tea steep in cream for at least 30 minutes.

7. Boil mixture once again and strain over the bowl with chocolate and butter. Let sit for about 2 minutes until chocolate and butter have started to melt and then whisk until smooth. Put ganache in the refrigerator until it is thick enough (but not too thick!) to spread over cupcakes. You can also wait until it cools and beat it with an electric beater for about 5–10 minutes for a lighter, creamier chocolate frosting.

CRÈME BRULÉE Cupcakes

Crème Brulée literally means 'burnt cream'. Basically, it is a vanilla custard that is chilled, sprinkled with sugar just before serving, and placed under a grill so that the sugar burns and forms a crust. There are many variations on the theme. Here is a cupcake one.

MAKES: **ABOUT 16 CUPCAKES**

375g plain flour
3 teaspoons baking powder
½ teaspoon salt, plus pinch for the egg whites
125g unsalted butter, room temperature
300g sugar
2 eggs, separated
240ml milk
3 tablespoons caramel syrup (the kind used for ice cream sundaes)
1 teaspoon vanilla extract

BROWN SUGAR FROSTING
300g soft dark brown sugar
150g granulated sugar
Pinch of salt
120ml milk
50g unsalted butter, cut into pieces
2 tablespoons golden syrup
2 teaspoons vanilla extract
Soft brown sugar for sprinkling

1. Preheat oven to 180°C/350°F/Gas Mark 4.

2. Mix flour, baking powder and salt together and set aside.

3. Cream butter and sugar together until light and fluffy. Add egg yolks, one at a time, mixing well after each addition. Alternately beat in dry ingredients and milk. Add caramel syrup and vanilla. Beat until smooth.

4. Beat egg whites with a pinch of salt until stiff but not dry. Gently fold whites into batter.

5. Spoon batter into cupcake papers, filling cups about ⅔ full. Bake for about 20 minutes or until a tester inserted into the centre comes out clean. Remove from oven and cool.

6. Mix all the frosting ingredients except the vanilla in a heavy saucepan over low heat. Slowly bring mixture to the boil, stirring constantly, and boil for 1 minute. Remove from heat and cool until just warm to the touch. Add vanilla and beat until thick enough to spread. Frost cooled cupcakes and sprinkle with soft brown sugar.

CUPCAKE TIP
You can substitute the vanilla in the cupcake batter with lavender extract, orange flower water or rose water to add your own individual touch.

THE ARLÉSIENNE

When I had my restaurant in the south of France, one of my most popular summer desserts was a tart made with fresh apricots, almonds and raspberry jam, known as the 'Arlésienne'. Arles is a lovely little city, located in Provence, on the banks of the Rhône river and in the middle of the Camargue, home to wild horses and pink flamingos. Provence abounds with apricot trees, almond trees, whose lovely pink blossoms announce the arrival of spring, and raspberries. The combination is definitely a winner.

MAKES: ABOUT 12 CUPCAKES

250g plain flour
2 teaspoons baking powder
1 teaspoon salt
125g unsalted butter, room
  temperature
100g sugar
2 eggs
5 tablespoons milk
Few drops of almond extract
  (optional)
75g dried apricots, or dried
  raspberries (or a combination of
  both), cut into little cubes
50g roughly ground almonds
6 small apricots, halved
12 teaspoons raspberry jam

1. Preheat oven to 180°C/350°F/Gas Mark 4.

2. Mix flour, baking powder and salt together and set aside.

3. Cream butter and sugar until light and fluffy. Add eggs, one at a time, mixing well after each addition. Alternately beat in flour mixture and milk. Add almond extract to taste. Fold in dried apricots and almonds.

4. Spoon batter into cupcake papers, filling a little over ½ full. Place an apricot half in the top of each cupcake, hollow side up, pressing gently into batter. Put a teaspoon of raspberry jam in each hollow. Bake for 20–25 minutes or until a tester inserted into the centre comes out clean and the tops are golden brown. Remove from oven and cool.

CUPCAKE TIP
The picture opposite depicts the cupcakes before they are baked. They should be a lovely golden colour when cooked.

PECHE MELBA Cupcakes

Try this very easy one-bowl cupcake version of the popular dessert. If you prefer you could bake the cupcakes in silicone moulds and serve with Raspberry Sauce and whipped cream.

MAKES: ABOUT 16 CUPCAKES

3 eggs, slightly beaten
300g sugar
120ml vegetable oil
300g plain flour
2 teaspoons baking powder
1 teaspoon salt
1 teaspoon cinnamon (optional)
350g fresh, tinned, or frozen peaches, cut into pieces (set aside enough thin slices to decorate cupcakes)

RASPBERRY CREAM FROSTING
240ml whipping cream, chilled
3 tablespoons sugar
120ml slightly sweetened raspberry purée (if you are using fresh raspberries, purée them with a fork or in a food processor with 1 tablespoon sugar)

RASPBERRY SAUCE
350g raspberries (set a few aside to decorate cupcakes)
100g sugar
60ml water
Few drops lemon juice
Whipped cream for decoration

1. Preheat oven to 180°C/350°F/Gas Mark 4.

2. In a large bowl, mix all of the cupcake ingredients apart from the peaches with a wooden spoon. Gently fold in peaches.

3. Spoon batter into cupcake papers, filling about ⅔ full. Bake for about 25 minutes or until a tester inserted into the centre comes out clean. Remove from oven and cool.

4. Make either Raspberry Whipped Cream Frosting or Raspberry Sauce. For frosting: beat cream with sugar until soft peaks form. Gradually add raspberry purée, beating continually. Beat until stiff peaks form. Add more sugar, if necessary. Frost cupcakes just before serving and decorate with a peach slice.

5. To make the sauce: wash and clean raspberries. Slowly heat raspberries and sugar in a medium pan with water. When mixture starts to boil, cook for 1 minute and remove from heat. Purée by hand or in a food processor with a few drops lemon juice. Spoon raspberry sauce over cupcakes. Serve with a dollop of whipped cream and a fresh raspberry.

CUPCAKE TIP
The Raspberry Sauce can be kept in the refrigerator or frozen for later use.

THE LANGUEDOCIENNE

Languedoc is a region in southern France known for its abundant sunshine, fields of lavender, figs, goat cheese, honey and great wines. These cupcakes embody the spirit of the region. Enjoy them after a meal with a glass of sweet Muscat wine.

MAKES: ABOUT 16 CUPCAKES

150g honey
100g soft light brown sugar
65g unsalted butter, cut into pieces
3 tablespoons milk
250g plain flour
2 teaspoons baking powder
1 teaspoon salt
1 tablespoon dried lavender
   (optional)
2 eggs
150g dried figs, cut into little pieces
   (save a few pieces for the
   decoration)

GOAT CHEESE FROSTING
180g very fresh goat cheese or
   creamy goat cheese such as
   Chavroux (can be found in most
   supermarkets)
30g unsalted butter, softened
225g icing sugar

1. In a medium saucepan, heat honey, sugar, butter and milk over very low heat. Stir until the sugar has dissolved and remove from heat. Leave to cool.

2. Preheat oven to 180°C/350°F/Gas Mark 4.

3. Mix flour, baking powder, salt and lavender together. Add to cooled honey mixture and beat well with a wooden spoon. Add eggs, one by one, beating well after each addition. Fold figs into batter.

4. Fill cupcake papers about ²/₃ full. Bake for about 25 minutes or until a tester inserted into the centre comes out clean.

5. To make the frosting: cream goat cheese, butter and sugar until smooth and well blended. If frosting is too soft or liquid, place it in the refrigerator until it is of good spreading consistency. Put a dollop of frosting on each cupcake and decorate with a piece of dried fig.

CUPCAKE TIP
If you can't get goat cheese, use cream cheese instead.

RICOTTA LIME
Cupcakes with Lime Glaze

These light and airy cupcakes will be as welcome as a lime cooler on a hot summer's day. You can dust them with icing sugar or use a lime glaze that will look very cool with a dollop of whipped cream, sprinkled with green sugar, and topped with a crystallized or jellied lime section.

MAKES: **ABOUT 16 CUPCAKES**

185g plain flour

1½ teaspoons baking powder

1 teaspoon salt, plus pinch for the egg whites

Juice (about 3 tablespoons) and finely grated rind of 1 lime

80g unsalted butter, room temperature

175g sugar

80g ricotta cheese

3 eggs, separated

LIME GLAZE

2 tablespoons freshly squeezed lime juice

75g icing sugar

FOR DECORATION

Whipped cream (optional)

Green sugar

Crystallized or jellied lime sections

1. Preheat oven to 180°C/350°F/Gas Mark 4.

2. Mix flour, baking powder, salt and lime rind together and set aside.

3. Cream butter and sugar together until light and fluffy. Add ricotta, beating until smooth. Add egg yolks, one at a time, blending well after each addition. Add flour mixture and lime juice and mix well.

4. Beat egg whites with a pinch of salt until stiff but not dry. Gently fold whites into batter.

5. Spoon batter into cupcake papers, filling cups about ⅔ full. Bake for about 20–25 minutes or until a tester inserted into the centre comes out clean. Remove from oven and cool.

6. To make the frosting: in a small bowl, combine lime juice and sugar and whisk until smooth. Spread over cooled cupcakes with a pastry brush. Decorate whipped cream with green sugar and a crystallized or jellied lime section.

TIRAMISU Cupcakes with Mascarpone Cream

Tiramisu is an Italian cake usually made with sponge cake or ladyfingers soaked in a mixture of coffee and Marsala, filled with mascarpone cream and topped with grated chocolate. Here is one cupcake version.

MAKES: ABOUT 12 CUPCAKES

150g plain flour
1 teaspoon baking powder
½ teaspoon salt
2 eggs, separated
60ml very strong coffee
1 tablespoon Marsala or 1 tablespoon
   Kahlua or 1 teaspoon vanilla
   extract
150g sugar
Pinch of salt
Extra Marsala for sprinkling (optional)

MASCARPONE CREAM
2 egg yolks
3 teaspoons sugar
1 tablespoon Kahlua (optional)
240g mascarpone
Kahlua for drizzling
Grated chocolate for decoration

1. Preheat oven to 180°C/350°F/Gas Mark 4.

2. Mix flour, baking powder and salt together and set aside.

3. Beat egg yolks with coffee and Marsala until very thick and creamy. Gradually add 110g of the sugar, beating continually. Set aside.

4. Beat egg whites with salt until they start to form moist peaks and gradually beat in remaining 40g sugar. Continue beating until egg whites are stiff but not dry. Stir 3 tablespoons of the whites into yolk mixture. Gradually fold dry ingredients into mixture, using a whisk. When the dry ingredients have been absorbed, gently fold in remaining whites.

5. Spoon batter into 12 cupcake papers, filling about ⅔ full. Bake for about 20 minutes or until a tester inserted into the centre comes out clean. Remove from oven and cool.

6. When cupcakes are cool, you can poke tops with a fork a few times and sprinkle a tablespoon of Marsala over each cupcake, if desired.

7. To make the mascarpone cream: beat egg yolks with sugar until they are light and fluffy. Beat in Kahlua, if desired. Gradually add mascarpone, beating continually. Pile cream on cupcakes, drizzle with kahlua and sprinkle with chocolate.

LINZERTORTE
Cupcakes

These cupcakes are an adaptation of a recipe from my friend Hannelore, who grew up on her Austrian mother's linzertortes, to which she added a touch of chocolate to give them more body.

MAKES: ABOUT 12 CUPCAKES

185g unsalted butter, room
  temperature
150g plain flour
½ teaspoon salt, plus good pinch for
  the egg whites
30g cocoa powder
225g icing sugar
100g ground almonds
100g ground hazelnuts
6 egg whites
Good pinch of salt
Raspberry jam (see method)
Whipped cream or decorator frosting
Hazelnuts or almonds, halved, for
  decoration
Icing sugar for dusting

1. Preheat oven to 180°C/350°F/Gas Mark 4.

2. In a small saucepan, melt butter, letting it brown just slightly. Remove from heat and cool.

3. In a large bowl, mix flour, salt, cocoa powder, icing sugar, ground almonds and hazelnuts together. Set aside.

4. Beat egg whites with a pinch of salt until they are foamy but not stiff.

5. Make a well in the middle of the dry ingredients and add egg whites and cooled butter. Mix well.

6. Spoon batter into cupcake papers, filling about ⅔ full. Bake for about 20–25 minutes or until a tester inserted into the centre comes out clean. Remove from oven and cool.

7. When cupcakes are cool, take out the centres with an apple corer and fill each cupcake with a teaspoon of raspberry jam. Replace core.

8. To glaze, heat 115g raspberry jam in a small pan over low heat. Brush on cooled and filled cupcakes with a pastry brush. Make criss-cross patterns on top of each cupcake with either whipped cream or a decorator tube. Put half a hazelnut or almond in each square and dust with a little icing sugar.

MENDIANT Cupcakes with Fig Topping

The term "mendiant" generally means beggar in French, but in the kitchen it refers to preparations made with dried fruits and nuts. Use your favourite one.

MAKES: ABOUT 16 REGULAR CUPCAKES OR 8 JUMBO CUPCAKES

75g hazelnuts
75g almonds
300g plain flour
2 teaspoons baking powder
1 teaspoon bicarbonate of soda
1 teaspoon salt
1 teaspoon cinnamon
1/2 teaspoon allspice
125g unsalted butter, room
  temperature
200g soft dark brown sugar,
  firmly packed
2 eggs
4 teaspoons white vinegar
160ml milk
75g raisins

FIG TOPPING
400g dried figs
375ml water
1 cinnamon stick
150g sugar

1. Place all of the topping ingredients in a heavy saucepan and bring to the boil. Lower heat and simmer for about 20 minutes or until the figs are tender and about half of the water has evaporated. Remove cinnamon stick and discard. Purée the fig mixture in a food processor. Set aside.

2. Preheat oven to 180°C/350°F/Gas Mark 4. Put hazelnuts and almonds in a dish in the oven and cook them until they are browned, about 10 minutes, stirring from time to time. Keep a close eye on them as you don't want them to burn. Roughly grind the nuts in a food processor and set aside.

3. Mix flour, baking powder, bicarbonate of soda, salt and spices. Set aside.

4. Cream butter and sugar until light and fluffy. Add eggs, one at a time, mixing well after each addition. Combine vinegar and milk. Alternately add dry ingredients and liquid, beating until smooth after each addition. Fold in raisins and ground nuts.

5. Spoon batter into regular or jumbo cupcake papers, filling cups just a little over 1/2 full. Cook for about 20 minutes, until just barely cooked. Remove from oven and spread fig mixture over each cupcake. Return to oven and cook for another 10 minutes or until cooked. Remove from oven and cool completely before unmoulding.

MARRAKECH Moments

I remember arriving in Marrakech at Christmas time with the orange trees heavy with fruit and the smell of orange flower blossom in the air. Thus, my inspiration for this dazzling duo.

MAKES: ABOUT 12 CUPCAKES

180g cream cheese, softened
50g sugar
2 tablespoons finely grated orange rind
1 tablespoon orange juice

CHOCOLATE BATTER
225g plain flour
2 teaspoons baking powder
1 teaspoon salt
200g sugar
50g unsweetened cocoa powder
120ml milk
80ml vegetable oil
1 egg
1 teaspoon vanilla extract

CHOCOLATE ORANGE GANACHE
180g dark chocolate, broken into little pieces
180ml double cream
3 tablespoons orange liqueur (Cointreau, Grand Marnier, etc.)

FOR DECORATION
Orange sugar or grated orange rind
Crystallized orange

1. Preheat oven to 180°C/350°F/Gas Mark 4. Mix the cream cheese, sugar, orange rind and orange juice in a bowl and set aside.

2. In a large bowl, mix flour, baking powder, salt, sugar and cocoa powder.

3. In a small bowl, mix milk, oil, egg and vanilla. Pour liquid into flour mixture and beat well with a wooden spoon.

4. Put a heaping tablespoon of the chocolate batter in the bottom of 12 cupcake papers. Divide up the orange cream cheese batter among the cupcakes (about a heaped teaspoon per cupcake).

5. Spoon over the remaining chocolate batter. Gently swirl batter with a knife (don't overdo it). Bake for 25–30 minutes or until a tester inserted into the centre comes out clean. Remove from oven and cool.

6. To make the ganache: place chocolate and cream in a bowl over a pan of simmering water, or in a microwave and heat until cream is warm to the touch and chocolate starts to melt. Remove from heat and stir until all of the chocolate has melted and the mixture is homogeneous. Remember, you don't want to cook the chocolate, you just want to melt it. You can always put it back over warm water or in the microwave for a few seconds if you need to. Stir in orange liqueur. Cool slightly then dip cupcakes in chocolate. The ganache will be smooth and shiny. Decorate with orange sugar or a piece of crystallized orange rind.

PINEAPPLE Surprises

The origin of this cupcake is a dessert that we used to serve at our restaurant. We were looking for something easy to put together and discovered this one on a trip to Spain and then adapted it to our taste. It actually consists of a regular size cupcake, topped with a mini-cupcake (with a brandied cherry hidden inside) and decorated to look like a pineapple.

MAKES: ABOUT 12 CUPCAKES

225g plain flour
2 teaspoons baking powder
1 teaspoon salt
185g unsalted butter
300g sugar
3 eggs
120ml juice (drained from pineapple)
1 small can crushed pineapple, drained (about 75g)
75g desiccated coconut
12 stoned brandied cherries or maraschino cherries

PINEAPPLE FONDANT GLAZE
225g icing sugar
2 tablespoons juice drained from pineapple
Yellow food colouring
Brown decorator frosting or caramel for decoration
Crystallized pineapple or pineapple sweets for decoration

1. Preheat oven to 180°C/350°F/Gas Mark 4.

2. Mix flour, baking powder and salt together and set aside.

3. Cream butter and sugar until light and fluffy. Add eggs, one at a time, mixing well after each addition. Alternately add dry ingredients and pineapple juice. When batter is well blended, fold in pineapple and desiccated coconut.

4. Spoon batter into 12 regular cupcake papers and 12 mini silicone moulds, filling cups about 1/2 full. Bake regular cupcakes for about 20–25 minutes and mini-cupcakes for a shorter time, or until a tester inserted into the centre comes out clean. Remove from oven and cool.

5. Turn cooled mini-cupcakes over and remove a little bit of the centre. Replace it with a brandied cherry.

6. To make the glaze: mix icing sugar and pineapple juice together until you obtain a smooth paste. Add yellow food colouring. Frost top of regular cupcakes. Place a mini-cupcake (with the cherry inside) on top while glaze is still soft. Ice. Decorate with brown decorator frosting or caramel to make the cupcake look like a pineapple. Place a piece of crystallized pineapple or a pineapple sweets on top.

MACADAMIA & WHITE CHOCOLATE Cupcakes

This cupcake recipe combines two ingredients with a unique flavour and texture – macadamia nuts and white chocolate.

MAKES: ABOUT 12–14 CUPCAKES

225g plain flour
2 teaspoons baking powder
1 teaspoon bicarbonate of soda
1 teaspoon salt
125g unsalted butter
175g sugar
2 eggs
120ml buttermilk
60g white chocolate chips
60g chopped macadamia nuts

WHITE CHOCOLATE FROSTING
120g good quality white chocolate
60ml double cream
180g cream cheese, room
   temperature
50g icing sugar

FOR DECORATION
Macadamia nuts, whole
Grated white chocolate

1. Preheat oven to 180°C/350°F/Gas Mark 4.

2. Mix flour, baking powder, bicarbonate of soda and salt together and set aside.

3. Cream butter and sugar until light and fluffy. Add eggs, one at a time, mixing well after each addition. Alternately add the dry ingredients and the liquid, beating until smooth after each addition. Fold in chocolate chips and macadamia nuts.

4. Spoon batter into cupcake papers, filling cups about ²⁄₃ full. Bake for about 20–25 minutes or until a tester inserted into the centre comes out clean. Remove from oven and cool.

5. To make the frosting: melt chocolate and cream in a bowl over a pan of simmering water, or in a microwave. Remove from heat when chocolate is just melted, stir and let cool. When mixture is cool to the touch, add cream cheese and icing sugar. Beat until mixture is thick and creamy. Frost cooled cupcakes and decorate with macadamia nuts and grated white chocolate.

ORIENT EXPRESS Cupcakes with Yin-Yang Frosting

East meets West in these lovely little green tea cupcakes. Enjoy them with a cup of green tea in the afternoon or for dessert after an Oriental-inspired meal.

MAKES: **ABOUT 12 CUPCAKES**

GREEN TEA CUPCAKE
150g plain flour
1 teaspoon baking powder
½ teaspoon salt, plus pinch for the
    egg whites
2 teaspoons powdered Japanese
    green tea
2 eggs, separated
100g icing sugar
50g ground almonds
100g unsalted butter, room
    temperature, cut into little pieces

YIN-YANG FROSTING
See Midnight Sky Frosting (page 76)

1. Preheat oven to 180°C/350°F/Gas Mark 4.

2. Mix flour, baking powder, salt and tea together and set aside.

3. In a large bowl, beat egg yolks with icing sugar until light in colour. Add ground almonds and beat well. Add butter and blend until mixture is smooth. Add dry ingredients and mix well. Beat egg whites with a pinch of salt until stiff but not dry and gently fold into batter.

4. Spoon batter into cupcake papers, filling about ⅔ full. Bake for about 20 minutes or until a tester inserted into the centre comes out clean. Remove from oven and cool.

5. Make the frosting according to the Midnight Sky Frosting recipe but before adding the black food colouring, divide the frosting into two bowls. Add black food colouring to one bowl and leave the other one white. Frost cooled cupcakes with a yin-yang design.

CUPCAKE TIP
You can also frost the cupcakes with ready-made fondant or one of the fondant recipes on page 142. Another possibility would be to decorate the cupcakes with a Chinese character.

MINI-FINANCIER
Cupcakes

A 'financier', which literally means exactly that in French, is a small cake that is made with ground nuts and whipped egg whites. A dab of apricot jam with some ground pistachios sprinkled on top and you will have a perfect accompaniment to a fruit salad or ice cream for dessert or a delicate finger cake for a 5 o'clock tea.

MAKES: ABOUT 24–30 MINI-CUPCAKES

150g plain flour
1 teaspoon baking powder
½ teaspoon salt, plus pinch for the egg whites
125g finely ground almonds
200g soft light brown sugar
5 egg whites
125g unsalted butter, melted and cooled
Several drops of almond extract
115g apricot jam
60g ground pistachio nuts

1. Preheat oven to 180°C/350°F/Gas Mark 4.

2. In a large bowl, combine the first five ingredients and set aside.

3. Beat egg whites with a pinch of salt until stiff but not dry. Fold into dry ingredients. Gradually add melted butter with a few drops of almond extract, gently folding it in with a whisk or a rubber spatula.

4. Spoon batter into mini-cupcake papers or silicone moulds, filling just a little over ½ full. Bake for about 20 minutes or until a tester inserted in the centre comes out clean. Remove from oven and cool.

5. In a small saucepan, melt apricot jam until just warm. Add a few drops of water, if necessary. Brush the jam on the cooled cupcakes with a pastry brush and sprinkle with ground pistachio nuts.

CUPCAKE TIP
You can bake them either in mini-cupcake papers or in a silicone mini-cupcake mould.

POIRE Belle Hélène

Here is another elegant French dessert transformed into a cupcake. A Poire Belle Hélène is usually vanilla ice cream served with a poached or ripe pear half and doused in chocolate sauce.

MAKES: **ABOUT 12 REGULAR CUPCAKES OR 6 JUMBO CUPCAKES**

150g plain flour
1 teaspoon baking powder
½ teaspoon salt, plus pinch for the egg whites
200g good quality dark chocolate (at least 55% cocoa solids)
125g unsalted butter
130g sugar
3 eggs, separated
3 pears (fresh or tinned), drained and cut into small pieces, plus 1 pear cut into lengthways slices for decoration

CREAMY CHOCOLATE SAUCE
100g sugar
1 tablespoon plain flour
Pinch of salt
360ml full fat milk
90g good quality dark chocolate (at least 55% cocoa solids), broken into pieces
30g unsalted butter, cut into little pieces
1 teaspoon vanilla extract

1. Preheat oven to 180°C/350°F/Gas Mark 4.

2. Mix flour, baking powder and salt together and set aside.

3. Melt chocolate with butter in a bowl over a pan of simmering water, or in a microwave. When just melted, remove from heat, stir well and add sugar to chocolate mixture. Mix thoroughly. Add egg yolks, one by one, mixing well after each addition, followed by dry ingredients. Beat batter until smooth and all of the flour has disappeared.

4. Beat egg whites with pinch of salt until stiff but not dry. Gently fold into batter. Chop 2 pears into small pieces and carefully add to batter.

5. Spoon batter into cupcake papers, filling cups about ⅔ full. Bake for about 25 minutes or until a tester inserted into the centre comes out clean. Remove from oven and cool.

6. To make the chocolate sauce (or use ready-made): in a small bowl, mix sugar, flour and salt together and set aside.

7. Heat milk and chocolate in a heavy saucepan over low heat until just melted. Stir with a wooden spoon until smooth. Add dry ingredients to chocolate mixture, mixing well. Simmer for 5 minutes, stirring constantly. Remove from heat and stir in butter and vanilla.

8. Spoon warm chocolate sauce over cupcakes or dribble a little over the top of each cupcake and decorate with a slice of the remaining pear.

WHITE CHOCOLATE & RASPBERRY Cupcakes

These easy and elegant cupcakes were inspired by a pie that a friend of mine once made with white chocolate, fresh raspberries, and decorated with real chocolate leaves.

MAKES: ABOUT 12–14 CUPCAKES

200g plain flour
1½ teaspoons baking powder
1 teaspoon salt
180g white chocolate, broken up into little pieces
125g unsalted butter, cut into little pieces
200g sugar
6 eggs
115g dried raspberries

RASPBERRY BUTTER CREAM FROSTING

250g icing sugar
240g unsalted butter, room temperature, cut into small pieces
Pinch of salt
2 tablespoons crème de framboise, raspberry liqueur or raspberry syrup
Chocolate leaves for decoration (see step 6)
Fresh or frozen raspberries for decoration

1. Preheat oven to 180°C/350°F/Gas Mark 4.

2. Mix flour, baking powder and salt together and set aside.

3. Melt chocolate and butter in a bowl over a pan of simmering water, or in a microwave. Remove from heat. Add sugar and mix well. Add eggs, one at a time, mixing well after each. Add dry ingredients. Fold in raspberries.

4. Spoon batter into cupcake papers, filling about ²⁄₃ full. Bake for about 20–25 minutes or until a tester inserted into the centre comes out clean. Remove from oven and cool.

5. To make the frosting: sift sugar into the large bowl of an electric mixer. Add butter and a pinch of salt. Beat on medium speed until frosting is light and fluffy. Add raspberry flavouring and continue beating until frosting is of good spreading consistency. Frost cooled cupcakes.

6. To make the chocolate leaves: melt about 240g dark chocolate in a bowl over a pan of simmering water, or in a microwave. Using a pastry brush, paint the undersides of leaves with the chocolate. You can use any non-toxic leaf (lemon or orange tree leaves). Place leaves on a piece of wax paper on a tray and put them in the refrigerator until chocolate has hardened (this will take only a few minutes). Very carefully peel off leaves.

7. Decorate frosted cupcakes with a few raspberries and chocolate leaves.

GATEAU DE SAVOIE
(Savoy Cake)

This cupcake is actually a very simple and basic sponge cake, that originated in the Savoy region of France, in the French Alps. The beauty of these cupcakes lies in their simplicity. You can add 75g of your favourite nuts or dried fruits, a few spoonfuls of coconut, a teaspoon of strong powdered espresso, etc. A very versatile cupcake, to say the least!

MAKES: ABOUT 12 REGULAR CUPCAKES AND 24–30 MINI-CUPCAKES

150g plain flour
1 teaspoon baking powder
½ teaspoon salt, plus pinch for the egg whites
125g unsalted butter, room temperature
150g sugar
4 eggs, separated
1 teaspoon vanilla extract
Icing sugar for dusting (optional)
Glaze or frosting of your choice

1. Preheat oven to 180°C/350°F/Gas Mark 4.

2. Mix flour, baking powder and salt together and set aside.

3. Cream butter with sugar until light and fluffy. Add egg yolks, one at a time, mixing well after each addition. Add the dry ingredients.

4. Beat egg whites with a pinch of salt until stiff but not dry. Gently fold into batter.

5. Spoon batter into cupcake papers, filling cups about ⅔ full. Bake for 20–25 minutes or until a tester inserted into the centre comes out clean. Cupcakes should be elastic to the touch. Remove from oven and cool.

6. Dust the cooled cupcakes with icing sugar, or glaze or frost them with the icing of your choice.

CUPCAKE TIP
You can either frost them, glaze them or dust them with icing sugar and serve with a fruit salad.

SAFFRON & ORANGE Cupcakes

These gourmet cupcakes with their delicate saffron threads and subtle flavours of orange and almond will be the perfect accompaniment to a 5 o'clock cream tea. Serve them with a bowl of fresh cream and a mug of black tea and enjoy. You won't be hungry for dinner.

MAKES: ABOUT 16–18 CUPCAKES

240ml freshly squeezed orange juice
1 tablespoon finely grated orange rind
$1/4$ teaspoon saffron threads (not powder)
3 eggs
150g icing sugar, plus more for dusting
250g plain flour
2 teaspoons baking powder
1 teaspoon salt
150g ground almonds
125g unsalted butter, melted

1. Preheat oven to 180°C/350°F/Gas Mark 4.

2. In a medium pan, bring orange juice, orange rind and saffron to the boil. Lower the heat and simmer for 1 minute. Remove from heat and cool.

3. In a large bowl, cream eggs and sugar until they are light and foamy. Add flour, baking powder, salt, almonds, orange juice mixture and butter, mixing ingredients in rapidly with a wooden spoon. The mixture may be a little lumpy.

4. Spoon batter into cupcake papers, filling $2/3$ full, and smoothing over with a spoon. Bake for about 25 minutes or until a tester inserted into the centre comes out clean. Remove from oven and cool.

5. Dust with icing sugar and serve with a bowl of thick fresh cream.

CUPCAKE TIP
You can also frost these cupcakes if you prefer. Try one of the orange frostings (Fresh Orange Juice Frosting, page 187, for example) and decorate with Caramelized Slivered Almonds (page 87).

STRAWBERRY Cheesecakes

A cheesecake in a cupcake! Is it possible? Not really, but a little imagination will go a long way and no one will be disappointed after they have tasted these scrumptious, delectable morsels with a surprise inside and strawberries and cream on top. Let them eat cupcakes!

MAKES: ABOUT 12 CUPCAKES

90g cream cheese
150g sugar
350g plain flour
2½ teaspoons baking powder
1 teaspoon salt
2 eggs, lightly beaten
240ml milk
30g unsalted butter, melted
1 tablespoon finely grated orange
   rind
12 small strawberries, hulled and
   cleaned, for the filling

STRAWBERRIES & CREAM FROSTING
1 egg white
Pinch of salt
240ml whipping cream
120g icing sugar
2 tablespoons strawberry liqueur or
   strawberry syrup
120ml strawberry purée

1. Preheat oven to 180°C/350°F/Gas Mark 4.

2. Mix cream cheese with 50g sugar and set aside.

3. In a large bowl, mix flour, baking powder, salt and the remaining 100g sugar.

4. In a separate bowl, beat eggs with milk and melted butter. Pour liquid into flour mixture and mix together rapidly with a wooden spoon. Blend in orange rind.

5. Put a heaping spoonful of the mixture into 12 cupcake papers (half the mixture). Place a strawberry and a teaspoonful of the cream cheese in the centre and cover with remaining mixture. Cook for 20 minutes in the oven. Remove and let cool before unmoulding.

6. To make the frosting: beat egg white with salt until stiff but not dry. Beat whipping cream separately until it forms soft peaks, then slowly beat in the sugar and strawberry flavouring. Fold two mixtures together. Gently fold in puréed strawberries. Just before serving, heap the cream on the cupcakes and decorate to your taste.

HOLIDAY
CUPCAKES

VALENTINE'S DAY Cupcakes

These filled cupcakes bring together one of the most divine duos known to chocolate lovers – chocolate and cherry – with a little cream thrown in for good measure.

MAKES: ABOUT 16 CUPCAKES

225g plain flour
75g cocoa powder
2 teaspoons baking powder
1 teaspoon bicarbonate of soda
1 teaspoon salt
125g unsalted butter
250g sugar
2 eggs
1 teaspoon vanilla extract
160ml soured cream

CHERRY CREAM CHEESE FILLING
180g cream cheese
3 tablespoons sugar
4 tablespoons Maraschino cherry
   syrup
Maraschino cherries or pitted
   brandied cherries

CHERRY JUBILEE FROSTING
60g unsalted butter
300g icing sugar
3 tablespoons Maraschino cherry syrup
Several drops red food colouring
   (optional)
Cocoa powder (about 2 tablespoons)
   for dusting
Maraschino cherries for decoration

1. Preheat oven to 180°C/350°F/Gas Mark 4.

2. Mix flour with cocoa, baking powder, bicarbonate of soda and salt. Set aside.

3. Cream butter and sugar until light and fluffy. Add eggs, one at a time, mixing well after each addition. Add vanilla. Alternately beat in flour mixture and soured cream.

4. Fill cupcake papers about ⅔ full. Bake for 25 minutes or until a tester inserted into the centre comes out clean. Remove from oven and cool.

5. To make the filling: using a fork or in a blender or mixer, mix cream cheese, sugar and cherry syrup together until smooth. You can use more syrup if necessary. Scoop out the centre of each cupcake with an apple corer. Drop in a teaspoon of filling and a cherry. Replace core. Save leftover filling for frosting.

6. To make the frosting: cream butter with any leftover filling until light and fluffy. Add icing sugar, cherry syrup and food colouring and beat until smooth and creamy. Add more cherry syrup if necessary. Frost filled cupcakes. Lightly dust with cocoa and place a cherry on the top of each cupcake.

CUPCAKE TIP
For a simpler alternative, use the Chocolate Fudge Icing for the Banana Split Cupcake (page 56).

EPIPHANY Cupcakes

The Feast of the Epiphany (also known as King's Day) celebrates the visit of the Three Wise Men to Bethlehem. In France today it is the unofficial ending of the holiday season.

MAKES: ABOUT 12 CUPCAKES

265g plain flour
2 teaspoons baking powder
1 teaspoon salt
125g unsalted butter
225g sugar
3 eggs
120ml milk
200g blanched almonds, finely chopped

ALMOND FILLING
125g marzipan, softened and cut into little pieces
90g cream cheese, room temperature
75g icing sugar
12 jelly beans or Jordan almonds

ALMOND BUTTER CREAM FROSTING
100g unsalted butter, room temperature
125g marzipan, softened and cut into little pieces
375g icing sugar
2 tablespoons milk
$\frac{1}{8}$ teaspoon almond extract
Jelly beans or Jordan almonds

1. To make filling: mix first three ingredients together (you can use a food processor, if necessary) and set aside. Preheat oven to 180°C/350°F/Gas Mark 4.

2. Mix together flour, baking powder and salt and set aside.

3. Cream butter and sugar together until light and fluffy. Add eggs, one at a time, mixing well after each addition. Alternately add dry ingredients and milk, beating until smooth. Fold in chopped almonds.

4. Fill 12 cupcake papers with half of the batter. Place a spoonful of filling in the centre of the batter with a jelly bean or Jordan almond. Cover with remaining batter. Bake for about 20 minutes or until a tester inserted into the centre comes out clean. Remove from oven and cool.

5. To make the frosting: cream butter and marzipan together until smooth (you can use a food processor, if necessary). Transfer to a large bowl, add sugar and beat until creamy. Gradually add milk and almond extract and continue beating. You can add a little extra milk for a softer frosting and more extract, if necessary.

6. Frost cooled cupcakes. Decorate with either jelly beans or Jordan almonds, three to a cupcake (for the Three Wise Men!). Alternatively, you can sprinkle the frosted cupcakes with caramelized slivered almonds (page 87). If you are using almond charms, be sure to warn your guests!

ST. PATRICK'S DAY
Pistachio Yogurt Cupcakes

St. Patrick's Day is marked by parades and fireworks, and symbolized by the shamrock, a three-leaved clover. So paint the town green with this little green gem of a cupcake.

MAKES: ABOUT 18 CUPCAKES

150g plain flour
1 teaspoon baking powder
1 teaspoon bicarbonate of soda
1 teaspoon salt
1 teaspoon ground cardamom
  (optional)
190g unsalted butter, room
  temperature
150g soft brown sugar
3 eggs
1 teaspoon vanilla extract
125ml whole yogurt
150g unsalted pistachios, roughly
  chopped (they can be roasted for
  more flavour)
Green food colouring (optional)

GREEN ICING

20g unsalted butter, melted
2 tablespoons hot milk
225g icing sugar
Flavouring (optional)
Green food colouring

1. Preheat oven to 180°C/350°F/Gas Mark 4.

2. Mix flour, baking powder, bicarbonate of soda, salt and ground cardamom together and set aside.

3. Cream butter and sugar until light and fluffy. Add eggs, one at a time, mixing well after each addition. Add vanilla and green food colouring, if using. Alternately beat in flour mixture and yogurt. Fold in pistachios.

4. Spoon batter into cupcake papers, filling cups about ⅔ full. Bake for 25 minutes or until a tester comes out clean. Remove from oven and cool.

5. To make the icing: mix butter with hot milk in a large bowl. Slowly beat in sugar until the icing is of good spreading consistency. If you are using flavouring (almond, vanilla, etc.), add it now. Add green food colouring, drop by drop, until you obtain the desired colour. Ice the cooled cupcakes and decorate to your taste.

CUPCAKE TIP
You could decorate white iced cupcakes with orange sugar (for Northern Ireland) and green sugar (for the Republic of Ireland), with a white stripe down the middle representing hope for peace between them.

ST. PATRICK'S DAY IRISH SODA BREAD Cupcakes

The oatmeal, caraway seeds and dried currants are typical of the traditional Irish recipe but this lighter version will definitely get you in the mood. Wash it down with a glass of Irish Whiskey or Bailey's Irish Cream and you may even see some leprechauns!

MAKES: ABOUT 16 CUPCAKES

300g plain flour
1 tablespoon oatmeal
2 teaspoons baking powder
2 teaspoons bicarbonate of soda
1 teaspoon salt
125g unsalted butter, room
    temperature
200g sugar
2 eggs
180ml buttermilk
75g dried currants or raisins
1 tablespoon caraway seeds
    (optional)

IRISH WHISKEY FROSTING
60g unsalted butter, room
    temperature
300g icing sugar
Pinch of salt
2 tablespoons Irish whiskey (or
    Bailey's Irish Cream)
Green food colouring (optional)
Green sugar for sprinkling

1. Preheat oven to 180°C/350°F/Gas Mark 4.

2. Mix dry ingredients together and set aside.

3. Cream butter and sugar until light and fluffy. Add eggs, one at a time, beating well after each addition. Alternately beat in flour mixture and buttermilk. Fold in currants or raisins and caraway seeds.

4. Spoon batter into cupcake papers, filling cups about ⅔ full. Bake for 25 minutes or until a tester inserted into the centre comes out clean. Remove from oven and cool.

5. To make the frosting: cream butter, sugar and salt until light and fluffy. Slowly add whiskey or Irish Cream (and food colouring, if you are using it) and beat until frosting is of good spreading consistency. Frost cooled cupcakes and sprinkle with green sugar.

CUPCAKE TIP
For a simpler non-alcoholic version, just dust with icing and green sugars.

MOTHER'S DAY FILLED ROSE Cupcakes

Say it with roses when you offer her these exquisitely delicate cupcakes made with rose water, filled with rose jam, petals and all, and topped with rose syrup frosting.

MAKES: **ABOUT 18 CUPCAKES**

400g plain flour
3 teaspoons baking powder
1 teaspoon salt
125g unsalted butter, room
   temperature
150g sugar
2 eggs
60ml rose syrup
240ml milk
Rose jam

ROSE SYRUP FROSTING
90g unsalted butter, room
   temperature
300g icing sugar
3 tablespoons rose syrup
½ teaspoon rose water (optional)
Red food colouring (optional)

1. Preheat oven to 180°C/350°F/Gas Mark 4.

2. Mix flour, baking powder and salt together and set aside.

3. Cream butter and sugar until light and fluffy. Add eggs, one at a time, mixing well after each addition. Alternately add dry ingredients and syrup and milk to butter mixture, blending well after each addition.

4. Spoon batter into cupcake papers, filling cups about ⅔ full. Bake for 25–30 minutes or until a tester inserted into the centre comes out clean. Remove from oven and cool.

5. When cupcakes are cool, take the centre out of each cupcake, using an apple corer. Drop a scant teaspoon of rose jam into the centre and replace cupcake core.

6. To make the frosting: cream butter with sugar until it is light and fluffy. Gradually add rose syrup, rose water and food colouring, beating continually until frosting is of good spreading consistency. Frost cooled cupcakes and decorate to your taste.

EASTER LEMON CHIFFON Cupcakes

Use bright Easter colours and decorate these cupcakes as if they were Easter eggs, using coloured sugars, little sweets, stencils etc. Have the kids pitch in and decorate their own.

MAKES: ABOUT 18 CUPCAKES

75g plain flour, sifted
Finely grated rind of 1 small lemon
6 egg whites
Pinch of salt or ½ teaspoon cream
  of tartar
200g sugar

EASTER EGG ICING

450g ready-to-use fondant or use
  one of the Fondant recipes
  (page 142)
Sugar syrup (if required)
Food colouring

FOR DECORATION

Coloured sugars
Easter motifs

1. Preheat oven to 180°C/350°F/Gas Mark 4. Mix flour and lemon rind and set aside.

2. Put the egg whites, salt or cream of tartar in a large bowl. Beat egg whites until stiff but not dry. You want them to be a little moist. Beat in sugar, little by little. Gradually fold in flour with a whisk. This is the only time I ever sift flour. It allows me to add it slowly and not to deflate the egg whites. Do not overmix. The batter will be gorgeous – like a meringue.

3. Spoon batter into cupcake papers using two soup spoons, filling a little over halfway. Cook for about 15–20 minutes until cupcakes are golden on top and spring back to the touch. Remove from oven and cool.

4. Prepare ready-to-use fondant, according to manufacturer's instructions, or one of the fondant recipes. This will probably require heating the fondant, either in a microwave or in a bowl over a pan of simmering water, until just melted. Overheating will spoil the glossy appearance and change the texture. Add enough sugar syrup to achieve the desired consistency. Pour the fondant into separate bowls, depending on the number of colours you wish to use. Add food colouring until you have obtained the desired colour. Either dip cupcakes into the fondant or ice using a knife. Decorate with coloured sugars and Easter motifs.

EASTER LAVENDER BUTTERFLY Cupcakes

A bouquet of flowers in a cupcake – lavender, poppy, rose and, with a little bit of luck, violet! Easter is the holiday that we all associate with the beginning of spring, so offer your friends and family a bouquet of flowers – with a butterfly on top.

MAKES: ABOUT 24–30 CUPCAKES

200g plain flour
2 teaspoons baking powder
1 teaspoon salt
125g unsalted butter, room
    temperature
150g sugar
2 eggs
1 teaspoon vanilla extract
125ml single cream
2 tablespoons dried lavender flowers
2 tablespoons poppyseeds for
    decoration
Several teaspoons of your favourite
    jam (strawberry, raspberry, etc.)

FILLING
240ml whipping cream, chilled
4 tablespoons sugar
½ teaspoon lemon extract or another
    flavouring
1 tablespoon grated lemon rind (if
    using lemon extract)

1. Preheat oven to 180°C/350°F/Gas Mark 4.

2. Mix flour, baking powder and salt together and set aside.

3. Cream butter and sugar until light and fluffy. Add eggs, one at a time, mixing well after each addition, followed by vanilla. Alternately beat in flour mixture and cream. Fold in lavender flowers.

4. Fill cupcake papers about ⅔ full. Bake for about 25 minutes or until a tester inserted into the centre comes out clean. Remove from oven and cool.

5. To make the filling: in a large bowl, beat whipping cream. When it starts to stiffen, gradually add sugar and beat until stiff peaks form. Add flavouring and lemon rind.

6. Cut off the top of each cupcake and set aside – this will be the butterfly. Using a sharp knife, carefully remove a little cone from the centre of each cupcake and fill with cream. Sprinkle with a few poppyseeds. Cut the top in half and place the halves on top of the cream to look like the wings of a butterfly. Put a little jam in between the two halves to look like the butterfly's body.

JULY 4TH RED VELVET
Cupcakes

It is hard to imagine why anyone would have thought of adding red food colouring to chocolate cake, but the final effect is quite dazzling – especially with a Red, White and Blue theme.

MAKES: ABOUT 18 REGULAR CUPCAKES OR 9 JUMBO CUPCAKES

300g plain flour
2 tablespoons cocoa powder
2 teaspoons baking powder
1 teaspoon bicarbonate of soda
1 teaspoon salt
125g unsalted butter, room temperature
300g sugar
2 eggs
1 teaspoon vanilla extract
1 teaspoon distilled white vinegar
1 tablespoon red food colouring
240ml buttermilk

AMERICAN PARFAIT ICING
125g white vegetable shortening (you can replace the shortening with butter but the icing won't be quite as "white")
1 tablespoon milk
½ teaspoon vanilla extract
250g icing sugar

1. Preheat oven to 180°C/350°F/Gas Mark 4.

2. Mix flour, cocoa, baking powder, bicarbonate of soda and salt together and set aside.

3. Cream butter and sugar together until light and fluffy. Add eggs, one at a time, mixing well after each addition. Blend in vanilla, vinegar and food colouring. Alternately add flour mixture and buttermilk and beat until batter is smooth.

4. Spoon batter into cupcake papers, filling about ⅔ full, and cook for 20–30 minutes or until a tester inserted into the centre comes out clean. Remove from oven and cool.

5. To make the icing: cream shortening with milk until it is creamy. Add vanilla. Gradually add sugar to shortening. Beat with an electric mixer until icing is pale, light and fluffy. You may need to add a little more milk to reach the desired consistency. Ice cooled cupcakes and decorate with coloured sugars, stencils, sparklers, etc.

CUPCAKE TIP
This icing is perfect for stencils and coloured sugars.

JULY 4TH BLUEBERRY & RASPBERRY Cupcakes

These red, white and blue cupcakes will warm a patriot's heart and a gourmet's stomach! Decorate them with fresh blueberries and raspberries, covered with a raspberry glaze, on a background of white fondant.

MAKES: ABOUT 12 REGULAR CUPCAKES OR 6 JUMBO

250g plain flour
2 teaspoons baking powder
1 teaspoon bicarbonate of soda
1 teaspoon salt
125g unsalted butter, room temperature
130g sugar
1 egg
240ml buttermilk
1 teaspoon vanilla extract
100g blueberries (fresh or frozen)
100g raspberries (fresh or frozen)
Icing sugar or white fondant glaze (see method)
115g raspberry jam for glaze
Raspberries and blueberries for decoration

1. Preheat oven to 180°C/350°F/Gas Mark 4.

2. Mix flour, baking powder, bicarbonate of soda and salt together and set aside.

3. Cream butter and sugar until light and fluffy. Add egg, buttermilk and vanilla and mix well. Stir in dry ingredients. Gently fold in the blueberries and raspberries. If you are using frozen fruit, don't defrost before using.

4. Spoon batter into cupcake papers, filling about ⅔ full. Bake for about 25 minutes or until the top of the cupcakes are golden brown. Remove cupcakes from oven. Cool completely before unmoulding.

5. Dust cooled cupcakes with icing sugar or ice cooled cupcakes with White Fondant Glaze (page 142) or ready-to-use fondant.

6. After cupcakes are iced, heat raspberry jam in a small saucepan until it is just liquid (do not cook). Remove from heat immediately. Place a few raspberries in the centre of the cupcakes (preferably while the fondant is still soft). Surround with blueberries. Using a pastry brush, apply raspberry jam to fruits. This will make them shiny and will hold them in place after glaze has cooled.

THANKSGIVING CARROT & CRANBERRY Cupcakes

These can be served for dessert as an alternative to pumpkin pie, after a Thanksgiving feast, and will be a welcome treat to kids and adults alike throughout the harvest season.

MAKES: **ABOUT 12 CUPCAKES**

150g plain flour
1 teaspoon baking powder
1 teaspoon salt
2 teaspoons cinnamon
$\frac{1}{2}$ teaspoon grated nutmeg
120ml vegetable oil
100g sugar
50g soft brown sugar
2 eggs
75g grated carrots
60g walnuts, chopped
75g dried cranberries

CINNAMON AND SPICE FROSTING
60g unsalted butter
180g cream cheese
1 cup icing sugar
1 teaspoon vanilla extract
1 teaspoon cinnamon
$\frac{1}{2}$ teaspoon ground ginger
$\frac{1}{2}$ teaspoon grated nutmeg
$\frac{1}{4}$ teaspoon ground cloves
Cinnamon for dusting

1. Preheat oven to 180°C/350°F/Gas Mark 4.

2. Mix flour, baking powder, salt and spices together and set aside.

3. Using an electric mixer or a wooden spoon, beat oil and both sugars until blended. Add eggs, one at a time, and beat until smooth. Add flour mixture and blend thoroughly. Fold in carrots, walnuts and cranberries.

4. Fill cupcake papers about $\frac{2}{3}$ full. Bake for 25–30 minutes or until a tester inserted into the centre comes out clean. Remove from oven and cool.

5. To make the frosting: cream butter and cream cheese together until light and fluffy. Gradually add icing sugar, beating until smooth. Add vanilla and spices and continue beating until frosting is of good spreading consistency. Frost cooled cupcakes, dust with cinnamon and decorate with to your taste.

CUPCAKE TIP
Fresh or frozen cranberries could be used as well.

THANKSGIVING APPLE CIDER Cupcakes

This cupcake is a perfect autumn dessert or snack. The cider gives the batter a certain lightness but if you prefer a non-alcoholic version, just use apple juice.

MAKES: ABOUT 12 CUPCAKES

225g plain flour
2 teaspoons baking powder
1 teaspoon salt
1 teaspoon cinnamon
125g unsalted butter, room temperature
130g sugar
2 eggs
180ml sweet cider
150g dried apples, cut into little pieces

APPLE FILLING
3–4 apples peeled, cored and chopped into small pieces
200g soft light brown sugar
100g unsalted butter, cut into small pieces
30ml water
1 teaspoon cinnamon
$\frac{1}{2}$ teaspoon salt
Cinnamon for dusting
Apple wedges (either dried or fresh)

1. Preheat oven to 180°C/350°F/Gas Mark 4.

2. Mix flour, baking powder, salt and cinnamon together and set aside.

3. Cream butter and sugar together until light and fluffy. Add eggs, one at a time, blending well after each addition. Alternately add cider and dry ingredients. When batter is thoroughly blended, fold in dried apples.

4. Spoon batter into cupcake papers, filling cups about $\frac{2}{3}$ full. Bake for about 25 minutes or until a tester inserted into the centre comes out clean. Remove from oven and cool.

5. When cupcakes are cool, scoop out the centre and heap full with Apple Filling or apple sauce. You can make your own or use the store-bought version. To make your own: combine all filling ingredients in a heavy saucepan and cook over low heat for about 5–10 minutes or until apples are soft. Remove from heat and crush apples with a fork. Cool before filling cupcakes.

6. Dust each cupcake with a little cinnamon and top with an apple wedge and walnut halves.

CUPCAKE TIP
Save the cupcake centres and freeze them. They will make wonderful Lamingtons (see recipe on page 178).

HALLOWEEN ORANGE JUICE Cupcakes

Orange juice is one of the main ingredients in both the cupcake and the frosting, so it will be both beautiful and healthy! The lovely orange glaze lends itself marvellously well to Halloween decorations – coloured sugars, stencils, etc.

MAKES: ABOUT 16 CUPCAKES

300g plain flour
2 teaspoons baking powder
1 teaspoon salt
125g unsalted butter, room
    temperature
200g sugar
2 eggs
Juice and finely grated rind of
    1 orange
1 tablespoon lemon juice
A few drops orange food colouring
    (optional)

ORANGE DECORATOR GLAZE
200g sugar
¼ cup cornflour
240ml orange juice (fresh, if possible)
1 teaspoon lemon juice
Pinch of salt
30g unsalted butter
Orange food colouring (optional)

1. Preheat oven to 180°C/350°F/Gas Mark 4. Mix flour, baking powder and salt and set aside.

2. Cream butter and sugar until light and fluffy. Add eggs, one at a time, mixing well after each addition.

3. Combine orange juice and lemon juice and add enough water to make ⅔ cup. Alternately add flour mixture and liquid. Add orange rind and beat batter until smooth. Add food colouring if you are using it.

4. Spoon batter into cupcake papers, filling cups about ⅔ full. Bake for 25 minutes or until a tester inserted into the centre comes out clean. Remove from oven and cool.

5. To make the glaze: combine sugar and cornflour in a pan over low heat. Gradually add orange and lemon juices and stir until well blended. Add salt and butter. Cook over low heat, stirring constantly until the mixture is thick and glossy. Remove from heat and cool. Add food colouring, if desired. Glaze the cooled cupcakes. Decorate with Halloween colours and themes.

HALLOWEEN PUMPKIN PECAN Cupcakes

This is a pumpkin pie in a cupcake. Offer them to trick-or-treaters when they come to your door or serve them at a Halloween party.

MAKES: ABOUT 16 CUPCAKES

250g plain flour
2 teaspoons baking powder
1 teaspoon salt
1 teaspoon cinnamon
½ teaspoon ground ginger
½ teaspoon grated nutmeg
¼ teaspoon ground cloves
125g unsalted butter, room temperature
150g soft brown sugar
2 eggs
2 teaspoons vanilla extract
250g cooked or tinned pumpkin
100g chopped pecans (or any type of nut, raisins or mini-marshmallows)

FRESH ORANGE JUICE FROSTING
60g unsalted butter, room temperature
300g icing sugar
1 tablespoon fresh orange juice
1 tablespoon grated orange rind
1 egg white
Pinch of salt

1. Preheat oven to 180°C/350°F/Gas Mark 4.

2. Mix flour, baking powder, salt and spices together and set aside.

3. Cream butter and sugar until light and fluffy. Add eggs, one at a time, mixing well after each addition. Add vanilla and pumpkin and beat until smooth. Add dry ingredients. Fold in pecans.

4. Spoon batter into cupcake papers, filling cups about ⅔ full. Smooth batter with the back of a spoon. Bake for 30 minutes or until a tester inserted into the centre comes out clean. Remove from oven and cool completely before unmoulding.

5. To make the frosting: cream butter and sugar until light and fluffy. Add orange juice and rind and continue beating. Beat egg white with a pinch of salt until stiff but not dry. Gently fold into mixture. Spread on cooled cupcakes and decorate to your taste.

CUPCAKE TIP
The orange frosting can be left as is or decorated for the occasion with a piece of crystallized orange peel or pumpkin seeds, coloured sugars, black decorator frosting, etc.

DAY OF THE DEAD CHOC CINNAMON Cupcakes

'Dia de los Muertos' is a festive Mexican event to honour the dead, celebrated in November. This recipe calls for typical Mexican chocolate (mixed with cinnamon and raw sugar).

MAKES: ABOUT 16 CUPCAKES

265g plain flour
2 teaspoons baking powder
1 teaspoon salt, plus pinch for the egg whites
1 teaspoon cinnamon
175g/2 disks Mexican chocolate
120ml milk
125g unsalted butter, room temperature
150g soft brown sugar
4 eggs, separated
1 teaspoon vanilla extract (Mexican, if possible)

CINNAMON BUTTER FROSTING
125g unsalted butter
300g icing sugar
1 tablespoon milk
1 teaspoon vanilla extract (Mexican, if possible)
1 teaspoon cinnamon

FOR DECORATION
Cinnamon or green and red sugars
Skulls and crossbones
Cinnamon sweets

1. Preheat oven to 180°C/350°F/Gas Mark 4. Mix dry ingredients together and set aside.

2. Melt chocolate and milk together in a bowl over a pan of simmering water, or in a microwave. As soon as the chocolate is melted, remove from heat, stir to blend, set aside and cool.

3. Cream butter and soft brown sugar until light and fluffy. Add egg yolks, one at a time, mixing well after each addition. Add chocolate mixture and vanilla and mix until completely blended. Add flour mixture in three parts, blending well until flour disappears.

4. Beat egg whites with a pinch of salt until they are stiff but not dry. Gently fold whites into batter. Spoon batter into cupcake papers, filling cups about ⅔ full. Cook for about 20–25 minutes or until a tester inserted into the centre comes out clean.

5. To make the frosting: cream butter and sugar until light and fluffy. Add milk, vanilla and cinnamon and continue beating until frosting is of a good spreading consistency. Spread over cooled cupcakes and decorate.

6. To decorate: sprinkle with cinnamon or green and red sugars, skulls and crossbones, marigolds, little cinnamon sweets, etc. Day of the Dead sugar heads can be found in Mexican speciality stores.

CHANUKAH HONEY HAZELNUT Cupcakes

Chanukah is the Jewish Festival of Lights and one of the most joyous holidays of the Jewish calender. These delicate hazelnut cupcakes will add a gourmet touch to that very ungourmet but oh-so-delicious traditional Chanukah meal of potato latkes with sour cream and apple sauce.

MAKES: ABOUT 12 CUPCAKES

160g unsalted butter, cut into pieces
100g honey
40g plain flour
150g sugar
100g powdered or ground hazelnuts
1 teaspoon salt, plus pinch for the
   egg whites
4 eggs, separated

HONEY GLAZE
2 tablespoons honey
1 tablespoon fresh lemon juice
75g icing sugar, plus more
   for dusting (optional)
Sweets (optional) for decoration

1. Preheat oven to 180°C/350°F/Gas Mark 4.

2. Melt butter and honey together in a pan and set aside.

3. Mix flour, sugar, hazelnuts and salt in a bowl and set aside.

4. Beat egg whites with a pinch of salt until stiff but not dry. Set aside.

5. Pour butter and honey into dry ingredients and stir vigorously with a wooden spoon. Add egg yolks and mix well. Gently fold in egg whites. Batter will be light and airy.

6. Spoon batter into 12 cupcake papers, filling a little over ½ full. Cook for 20–25 minutes or until a tester inserted into the centre comes out clean. Remove from oven and cool.

7. To make the glaze: heat honey in a small pan until it is just warm. Gradually add honey and lemon juice to sugar, stirring to blend. Spread on cooled cupcakes and let cool. Place a candle in the centre of each cupcake before serving. Alternatively, dust the cooled cupcakes with icing sugar.

CHRISTMAS PEPPERMINT CHOCOLATE Cupcakes

These Christmas cupcakes will definitely evoke unforgettable visions of candy canes. Serve them as part of a Christmas buffet and throughout the holiday season.

MAKES: ABOUT 18 CUPCAKES

240ml water

4 peppermint tea bags

300g plain flour

2 teaspoons baking powder

1 teaspoon bicarbonate of soda

1 teaspoon salt, plus pinch for the egg whites

75g dark chocolate

300g sugar

125g unsalted butter, cut into small pieces

2 eggs, separated

120ml soured cream or buttermilk

PEPPERMINT CANDY FROSTING

120g cream cheese, softened

1 tablespoon milk

Pinch of salt

A few drops of mint extract

375g icing sugar

35g crushed peppermint sweets or sticks

Miniature peppermint candy canes or green and red sugar for decoration

1. Preheat oven to 180°C/350°F/Gas Mark 4.

2. Boil water in a small pan and add tea bags. Let steep for about 10 minutes. Remove tea bags and discard.

3. While tea is steeping, mix flour, baking powder, bicarbonate of soda and salt together and set aside.

4. In a bowl over a pan of simmering water, place mint tea, chocolate, sugar and butter. Stir until chocolate and butter have melted and mixture is smooth (you can use a microwave, if you prefer). Remove from heat and whisk in egg yolks, beating well. Alternately add flour mixture and soured cream or buttermilk and beat until batter is smooth.

5. Beat egg whites with a pinch of salt until they are stiff but not dry and gently fold into batter.

6. Spoon batter into cupcake papers, filling cups about ⅔ full. Bake for 25 minutes or until a tester inserted into the centre comes out clean. Remove from oven and cool.

7. To make the frosting: in a large bowl, blend cream cheese, milk, salt and mint extract and beat well. Gradually blend in icing sugar until smooth and creamy. Fold in crushed sweets. Spread on cooled cupcakes and decorate with a miniature candy cane and green and red sugar.

CHRISTMAS FRUIT
Cupcakes with White Fondant

These cupcakes are a cross between a Christmas pudding and a fruit cake, with a dash of brandy to warm your heart on a cold Christmas Eve.

MAKES: ABOUT 12 REGULAR CUPCAKES OR 6 JUMBO CUPCAKES

200g crystallized fruits
80ml brandy
300g plain flour
150g soft light brown sugar
2 teaspoons baking powder
1 teaspoon salt
1 teaspoon allspice
1 teaspoon ground cinnamon
1/2 teaspoon ground ginger
1/2 teaspoon grated nutmeg
120ml milk
1 egg, slightly beaten
2 tablespoons apricot jam
1 teaspoon finely grated orange rind
1 teaspoon finely grated lemon rind
125g unsalted butter, melted and
   cooled

WHITE FONDANT GLAZE
150g icing sugar
1 teaspoon finely grated lemon rind
1 tablespoon lemon juice

1. In a bowl, mix fruits and brandy and let stand for about 2 hours, stirring from time to time.

2. Preheat oven to 180°C/350°F/Gas Mark 4.

3. In a large bowl, mix flour, sugar, baking powder, salt and spices together and set aside.

4. Lightly beat the milk with the egg, apricot jam, orange and lemon rinds and melted butter. Add to flour mixture and mix well. Stir in fruits and brandy.

5. Spoon batter into cupcake papers, filling about ²⁄₃ full, and cook for 20–30 minutes, or until a tester inserted into the centre comes out clean. Remove from oven and cool.

6. To make the fondant glaze: mix icing sugar and lemon rind together and gradually add lemon juice until you obtain a smooth paste, easy to spread. You may not need all of the lemon juice. Glaze and decorate cupcakes to your taste.

CUPCAKE TIP
You can use either the fondant glaze recipe or ready-to-use fondant.

NEW YEAR'S EVE PINK CHAMPAGNE Cupcakes

There's nothing like champagne to usher out the old year and bring in the new one! Top these light and delicious cupcakes with a champagne popper and welcome in the New Year in style.

MAKES: ABOUT 16 CUPCAKES

300g plain flour
2 teaspoons baking powder
$\frac{1}{2}$ teaspoon salt
125g unsalted butter, room
    temperature
350g sugar
180ml pink champagne
Red food colouring (optional)
6 egg whites
Pinch of salt or cream of tartar

CHAMPAGNE FROSTING

190g unsalted butter, room
    temperature
300g icing sugar
2 tablespoons champagne
Red food colouring (optional)
Mini champagne poppers for
    decoration

1. Preheat oven to 180°C/350°F/Gas Mark 4.

2. Mix dry ingredients together and set aside.

3. Cream butter and sugar until light and fluffy. Alternately beat in flour mixture and champagne, blending well after each addition. Add food colouring, if desired.

4. Beat egg whites with a pinch of salt or cream of tartar until stiff but not dry and gently fold into batter.

5. Fill cupcake papers about $\frac{2}{3}$ full. Bake for 25–30 minutes or until a tester inserted into the centre comes out clean. Remove from oven and cool.

6. To make the frosting: beat butter and sugar until soft and creamy. Slowly add champagne and red food colouring, if desired and continue beating until frosting is of good spreading consistency. You can add more champagne for a softer frosting. Frost cooled cupcakes and decorate with a champagne popper.

CUPCAKE TIP
If you prefer not to use alcohol, you can use strawberry fizzy drinks instead of champagne to obtain the same effect.

NEW YEAR'S EVE CONFETTI Cupcakes

Welcome the New Year in with confetti. The crushed candies in the cupcakes will look like confetti when you bite into them.

MAKES: ABOUT 12 REGULAR CUPCAKES OR 24 MINI-CUPCAKES

150g plain flour

1 teaspoon baking powder

1 teaspoon salt

100g unsalted butter, room
temperature

100g sugar

3 eggs

1 tablespoon brandy or 1 teaspoon
vanilla extract

80g single cream

35g crushed mints or hard sweets of
different colours

4-MINUTE CONFETTI FROSTING

1 egg white

150g sugar

Pinch of salt

3 tablespoons water

1 teaspoon golden syrup

1 teaspoon vanilla extract or
1 tablespoon brandy

Confetti sweets (can be found in the
baking section of supermarkets)

1. Preheat oven to 180°C/350°F/Gas Mark 4.

2. Mix flour, baking powder and salt together and set aside.

3. Cream butter and sugar until light and fluffy. Add eggs, one at a time, mixing well after each addition, followed by brandy or vanilla. Alternately beat in flour mixture and cream. Fold in crushed sweets.

4. Fill cupcake papers about ⅔ full. Bake for about 20 minutes or until a tester inserted into the centre comes out clean. Remove from oven and cool.

5. To make the frosting: place egg white, sugar, salt, water and golden syrup in a bowl. Beat for about 1 minute until thoroughly mixed. Place the bowl over boiling water and beat at high speed for about 4 minutes or until frosting forms stiff peaks. Remove from heat and transfer to a large bowl. Add vanilla or brandy and beat for another minute or until of good spreading consistency. Frost cooled cupcakes and sprinkle confetti sweets over cupcakes before frosting hardens.

CUPCAKES
PLUS

DESSERT ROSE
Cupcakes

I originally put this 'cupcake' in the Kids section since it will certainly be a great favourite with them. But after writing the introduction to this book, I realized that it really doesn't fit my 'strict' definition of a cupcake so I moved it here. It doesn't require any cooking and can be made with little or no help from an adult. It is perfect for a party or just a snack and can be whipped up in the blink of an eye. The kids will love this one!

MAKES: ABOUT 12 REGULAR CUPCAKES OR 24 MINI-CUPCAKES

240g milk or dark chocolate, broken into pieces
200g unsalted butter, room temperature, cut into pieces
200g icing sugar
150g corn flakes

1. Melt chocolate and butter in a large bowl set over simmering water. Mix well.

2. Stir in icing sugar. Add corn flakes and mix gently until all of the corn flakes are coated with chocolate.

3. Spoon mixture into mini- or regular cupcake papers and set in the refrigerator for a few hours. Remove from refrigerator and enjoy.

CUPCAKE TIP
You can replace the milk or dark chocolate with white chocolate and the corn flakes with Rice Krispies, Special K or similar types of breakfast cereals.

ALMOND & HAZELNUT
Mini-Meringues

These mini-meringues are made in mini-silicone cupcake moulds. They can be eaten as is, served with fruit salad or ice cream or used with other desserts. They are easy to make and versatile in addition to being absolutely delicious.

MAKES: ABOUT 30 MINI-MERINGUES CUPCAKES

50g ground almonds
50g ground hazelnuts
150g sugar
5 egg whites
Pinch of salt
85g hazelnuts or almonds, toasted and coarsely chopped
Icing sugar for dusting

CUPCAKE TIP
They can be kept at room temperature for several days in a sealed container or frozen for future use.

1. Preheat oven to 170°C/325°F/Gas Mark 3.

2. Mix ground almonds, ground hazelnuts and 50g of the sugar together. Set aside. If you prefer, you can just use almonds, just hazelnuts or any combination of either.

3. Beat egg whites with salt until they turn opaque. Gradually add remaining sugar and continue to beat whites until they are stiff and form glossy peaks. Gently fold in ground nut mixture, using a whisk or a rubber spatula. I start with the whisk and finish with the spatula. Take care not to overmix.

4. Fill the mini-cupcake moulds with the mixture. You can use a piping bag to do this if you wish but if not, just heap the mixture into the moulds. Sprinkle the toasted nuts over the mini-meringues, pressing them in gently. Lightly dust with icing sugar. Let the meringues rest for 10 minutes and then dust them again with icing sugar and let them rest another 10 minutes.

5. Bake for about 25–30 minutes or until they are golden brown and firm to the touch. Cool before unmoulding.

DEEP-DISH APPLE PIE
Cupcakes

Deep-Dish Apple Pie is an all-American favourite and for good reason. These cupcakes work particularly well in silicone moulds, either the regular or jumbo version. Serve them on individual plates with a wedge of sharp cheddar cheese or a dollop of whipped cream.

MAKES: **ABOUT 8 REGULAR CUPCAKES OR 4 JUMBO CUPCAKES**

PIE DOUGH
See Chocolate Cupcake Pie
 (page 152)

APPLE PIE FILLING
4–5 apples, peeled, cored and
 cut into pieces
1 tablespoon lemon juice
100g sugar, plus 2 tablespoons extra
 for sprinkling
Pinch of salt
Dash of grated nutmeg
1 teaspoon cinnamon
2 tablespoons plain flour
65g unsalted butter, room
 temperature

1. Preheat oven to 230°C/450°F/Gas Mark 8.

2. See Chocolate Cupcake Pie (page 152) for instructions on rolling out pie dough and lining moulds. Serve enough dough to cut circles to cover the cupcakes.

3. In a large bowl, toss apples with lemon juice, 100g of the sugar, salt, nutmeg, cinnamon and flour, coating evenly. Scoop mixture into pie shells and dot with butter. Cover each cupcake with a circle of dough, crimping the edges for a pretty effect. Cut two vents into the top of each cupcake so that the steam can escape and sprinkle with remaining sugar.

4. Bake in the oven for 10 minutes and then turn down heat to 180°C/350°F/Gas Mark 4. Cook for another 15–20 minutes or until pie crust is golden brown. Cool cupcakes completely before removing from moulds.

VARIATION: DEEP-DISH PEACH PIE CUPCAKE

Substitute peaches for apples and cut into slices. Use just a pinch of cinnamon.

VARIATION: DEEP-DISH BLUEBERRY PIE CUPCAKE

Substitute blueberries for apples. Leave out cinnamon.

CHOCOLATE
Cupcake Pies

The inspiration for this cupcake was a pie that I used to make for my restaurant, itself inspired by a recipe from Bernachon, the great 'chocolatier' from Lyon. When I was testing the recipe, I just naturally assumed that I would have to use silicone moulds but my experiments proved that it was possible to make the cupcakes in cupcake papers as well.

MAKES: ABOUT 14–16 CUPCAKES

PIE DOUGH
Enough pie dough (any type – basic, flaky, etc.), homemade or ready-made to make two 23cm pies.
Plain flour for dusting

CHOCOLATE FILLING
125g good quality dark chocolate, broken into small pieces
450ml double cream
130g sugar
5 eggs

FOR DECORATION
Walnut halves (optional)
Whipped cream (optional)

1. Preheat oven to 180°C/350°F/Gas Mark 4.

2. Roll out the pie dough on a lightly floured surface and cut out circles measuring 10cm in diameter. Line silicone cupcake moulds or cupcake papers, folding the edge of the dough back under so that it will look pretty. Make a few holes in the bottom of the dough so that it doesn't buckle when cooked. Be gentle!

3. Melt chocolate in a large bowl set over a saucepan of simmering water. Remove from heat as soon as it is melted (do not cook). Add cream, sugar and eggs and beat until all of the ingredients are totally blended.

4. Carefully pour chocolate mixture into pie shells, filling about ¾ full. Bake for about 25 minutes or until chocolate is cooked. The filling will rise while cooking but will fall when it cools. Cool cupcakes completely before removing from moulds.

5. Decorate with a walnut half or a dollop of whipped cream, or both. If you are making the cupcakes in the silicone moulds, serve them in pretty cupcake papers.

CHERRY ALMOND PIE Cupcakes

Although you can use just about any filling for pie cupcakes, this is one of my favourites. I had it for the first time when I was visiting my cousin Iris in Monkton, Maryland, after a dinner of steamed Chesapeake Bay crabs and homemade coleslaw.

MAKES: ABOUT 14–16 CUPCAKES

PIE DOUGH
See Chocolate Cupcake Pie
    (page 152).

CHERRY ALMOND FILLING
125g unsalted butter, room
    temperature
100g sugar
2 large eggs
100g ground almonds
Finely grated rind of 1 lemon
325g stoned morello cherries (tinned
    cherries work wonderfully well but
    you can use fresh or frozen,
    depending on the season)
Icing sugar for dusting
Slivered almonds for decoration

1. Preheat oven to 180°C/350°F/Gas Mark 4.

2. See Chocolate Cupcake Pie (page 152) for instructions on rolling out pie dough and lining moulds.

3. Beat butter and sugar together until light and fluffy. Add eggs, one by one, beating well after each addition. Add ground almonds and lemon rind and mix well. Spoon mixture into pie shells, filling them about ½ full. Press the cherries into the mixture, pushing them under the almond paste with your fingers.

4. Bake for 25–30 minutes until the surface is golden brown, puffed up and springy to the touch. Turn off oven and leave cupcakes with door open for about 10 minutes. Remove from oven and leave to cool. Dust with icing sugar and decorate with slivered almonds before serving.

BAKLAVA Cups

The inspiration for these cupcakes is a wonderful and elegant dessert, found throughout North Africa and in every country around the Mediterranean basin.

MAKES: ABOUT 12 CUPCAKES

150g nuts (either walnuts, pistachios, or almonds, or a combination)
60g toasted sesame seeds
1 teaspoon cinnamon
½ teaspoon cardamom
½ cup honey
1 tablespoon lemon juice
1 teaspoon orange blossom or rose water
225g filo pastry dough
125g unsalted butter, melted and slightly cooled

1. Preheat oven to 180°C/350°F/Gas Mark 4.

2. Coarsely chop nuts in a food processor. Transfer to a medium bowl and add sesame seeds, cinnamon and cardamom. Mix well.

3. In a small saucepan, heat honey with lemon juice and orange blossom or rose water until just liquid and luke warm to the touch (do not cook). Pour mixture over nuts and stir well.

4. Cut filo dough into 12cm squares. Put a square into each regular-size silicone cupcake mould. Brush with melted butter. Repeat five more times for each cupcake, staggering the corners of the square so that the sides of the moulds are entirely covered. Flatten dough with the pastry brush as you go along. Put a heaped tablespoon of the nut and honey mixture in the centre of each cupcake. Using scissors or a very sharp knife, trim off excess dough to edge of cupcake moulds or leave as is.

5. Bake for about 15–20 minutes until mixture is brown on top and dough is cooked. Remove from oven and cool. Carefully unmould Baklava Cups. They will harden as they cool in the mould. Serve in pretty cupcake papers.

CUPCAKE TIP
Enjoy them with a cup of espresso or a glass of sweet mint tea after a meal or at tea time.

WHITE CHOCOLATE PANNA COTTA Cupcakes With Passion Fruit Sauce

Panna Cotta is an Italian egg cream that literally means 'cooked cream'. Technically, this recipe is not a real panna cotta since it calls for gelatin instead of egg yolks to set the cream. But this is a 'no fail' recipe, easy to make and delicious served with Passion Fruit Sauce or a simple fruit sauce of your choice. If you have any fancy silicone cupcake moulds with a design on top (sunflowers, roses, etc.), they would work particularly well.

MAKES: ABOUT 8–10 CUPCAKES

PANNA COTTA
300ml double cream
180ml full fat milk
150g white chocolate, broken into
    pieces
50g sugar
2 teaspoons unflavoured gelatin
1 tablespoon water

PASSION FRUIT SAUCE
120g passion fruit pulp
240ml sweet white wine (Sauternes
    or Muscat, for example)
50g sugar

1. In a medium pan, mix the cream, milk, chocolate and sugar. Gently heat mixture, stirring constantly, until it is smooth (do not boil).

2. Heat gelatin and water in a large bowl set over simmering but not boiling water or a microwave. Stir until gelatin has dissolved and add to chocolate mixture.

3. Divide mixture between 8–10 silicone cupcake moulds. Place in the refrigerator for about 3 hours until cream has set.

4. While cream is setting, mix the passion fruit pulp, wine and sugar in a small saucepan. Bring to the boil, lower heat and simmer for about 10 minutes without stirring, until mixture is reduced by about a third. Remove from heat and cool.

5. Unmould the panna cotta on individual plates and serve with Passion Fruit Sauce.

BABA AU RHUM
Cupcakes

These individual rum cakes are delicious with tea and make an elegant dessert, served with whipped cream or custard sauce. Use any size mould, depending on the desired effect. Mini-moulds can be used to make bite-size baba that may be a bit messy to eat, but your guests will go away licking their fingers – and complimenting the chef!

MAKES: ABOUT 12 CUPCAKES

125g plain flour
2 teaspoons baking powder
½ teaspoon salt, plus pinch for the
    egg whites
3 eggs, separated
125g sugar
6 tablespoons hot milk
60g unsalted butter, room
    temperature
1 teaspoon vanilla extract

SYRUP
450ml water
150g sugar
6 tablespoons rum
1 teaspoon vanilla extract

1. Preheat oven to 180°C/350°F/Gas Mark 4.

2. Mix flour, baking powder and salt together and set aside.

3. Using a mixer, cream egg yolks with sugar until the mixture is creamy and light in colour. While the mixer is running, add hot milk, flour mixture and butter and mix well. Add vanilla.

4. In a separate bowl, beat egg whites with a pinch of salt until stiff but not dry. Gently fold whites into batter. Pour batter into cupcake moulds immediately, filling just ½ full. Cook for about 20 minutes or until brown on top. Leave babas in moulds.

5. To make the syrup: in a medium saucepan, bring water and sugar to the boil and cook for 2 minutes. Remove from heat and add rum and vanilla. Slowly pour over babas, until all of the liquid is absorbed. Keep babas in their moulds until they are to be served so that they soak up a maximum of syrup. You can keep them in the refrigerator for a few days after they have cooled but serve them at room temperature with a dollop of whipped cream or on a bed of custard sauce.

BLUEBERRY TART
Cupcakes

Once again, this pie was a great favourite at my
restaurant. I usually made it in the autumn with the fresh
blueberries from the mountains nearby that inundated
the village market at that time of the year. But frozen
blueberries work at any time of the year.

**MAKES: ABOUT 14–16 REGULAR
CUPCAKES OR 7–8 JUMBO
CUPCAKES**

PIE DOUGH
See Chocolate Cupcake Pie (page
    152).

BLUEBERRY FILLING
350g blueberries (if you are using
    frozen blueberries, don't defrost
    them)
240ml double whipping cream
100g sugar
3 eggs
1 teaspoon vanilla extract
Whipped cream (optional)

1. Preheat oven to 180°C/350°F/Gas Mark 4.

2. See Chocolate Cupcake Pie (page 152) for instructions on rolling out
pie dough and lining moulds. For jumbo moulds cut out circles measuring
10cm in diameter.

3. Divide blueberries up among pie shells, filling shells no more than
$\frac{1}{2}$ full.

4. Beat cream, sugar, eggs and vanilla together. Pour mixture over
blueberries, filling shells about $\frac{2}{3}$ full. Bake for
about 25 minutes or until cream has set.
Cool cupcakes completely before
removing from moulds.

5. Serve with a dollop of whipped
cream. If you are making the cupcakes in
the silicone moulds, serve them in pretty
cupcake papers.

CUPCAKE TIP
*You can either
use silicone moulds or
cupcake papers.
Either work well.*

STRUDEL Cups

Strudel is said to be a Viennese speciality but can be found throughout Eastern Europe. I personally believe that it is the first cousin of baklava, probably brought to Europe by the Turks during the reign of the Ottoman Empire. It is generally made with apples but works well with cherries, ricotta cheese, apricots or poppyseeds, just to name a few possible ingredients. Here are a few different recipes that you can try.

MAKES: **ABOUT 12 CUPCAKES**

STRUDEL DOUGH
225g filo pastry dough
125g melted butter and slightly cooled

APPLE FILLING
4 medium apples peeled, cored and chopped
2 tablespoons lemon juice
100g sugar (more or less to taste)
60g walnuts, chopped
25g raisins
1 teaspoon cinnamon
25g browned bread crumbs or ground almonds
Whipped cream (optional)

1. Preheat oven to 180°C/350°F/Gas Mark 4.

2. Line regular silicone moulds with the filo pastry according to the directions for Baklava Cups (page 155).

3. To make the filling: place apple pieces in a large bowl. Add lemon juice and coat apples well so that they don't turn brown. Add remaining filling ingredients and mix well. The purpose of the bread crumbs or ground almonds is to absorb the liquid. Proceed as with Baklava Cups using this filling.

4. Serve individually on a plate with a dollop of whipped cream.

VARIATION: CHERRY FILLING

250g stoned sour cherries, fresh or frozen and defrosted (you can use any type of cherry but the sour ones work the best), 100g sugar (more or less to taste), 60g ground almonds, 1 teaspoon cinnamon.

VARIATION: RICOTTA FILLING

360g ricotta cheese (you can substitute with cottage cheese), 50g sugar, 1 egg, slightly beaten, 3–5 tablespoons raisins, 2 teaspoons finely grated lemon or orange rind.

BOSTON CREAM
Cupcakes

This cupcake is a variation of a Boston Cream Cake. The principle is two layers of a basic white cake, filled with custard, open on the sides (and a bit oozy!) and frosted on top.

MAKES: **ABOUT 18 REGULAR CUPCAKES OR 9 JUMBO CUPCAKES**

300g plain flour
2 teaspoons baking powder
1 teaspoon salt
125g unsalted butter, room temperature
200g sugar
3 egg yolks, well beaten
180ml milk
1 teaspoon vanilla extract

VANILLA CUSTARD FILLING
(CRÈME PATISSIÈRE)
360ml milk
1 vanilla pod (or 1 teaspoon vanilla extract)
100g sugar
35g plain flour
2 eggs, plus 2 yolks
Chocolate Ganache (page 81)

1. Preheat oven to 180°C/350°F/Gas Mark 4.

2. Mix flour, baking powder and salt together and set aside.

3. Cream butter and sugar until light and fluffy. Add egg yolks all at once and blend well. Alternately beat in dry ingredients and milk. Add vanilla.

4. Spoon batter directly into silicone cupcake moulds, filling about $^2/_3$ full. Bake for 20–25 minutes or until a tester inserted in the centre comes out clean. Remove from oven and cool.

5. To make the filling: in a small saucepan, heat milk with vanilla. When milk boils, remove from heat. Just before you are ready to use the milk, remove the vanilla pod, split it in half lengthways and scrape out the seeds inside into the milk. Discard the pod.

6. In a large bowl, combine sugar, flour, eggs and yolks and whisk until light and creamy. Place the bowl over a saucepan of simmering water and slowly add milk, stirring continually, and cook until mixture just starts to boil. Remove from heat and continue stirring for a few minutes to release steam and prevent mixture from continuing to cook. Leave to cool before using.

7. Cut cupcakes in half. If you are using jumbo cupcakes, you can even cut them in thirds. Fill with Vanilla Custard Filling and ice the tops of the cupcakes with Chocolate Ganache.

CARAMEL VERMICELLI
Cupcake Flans

No, it isn't your imagination! You heard right. Cupcake flans made with vermicelli, the same pasta you put in your soup. Imagine the look on your guests' faces when you tell them what the main ingredient is!

MAKES: ABOUT 16 CUPCAKES

50g raisins
2 tablespoons rum
1 litre full fat milk
200g sugar
175g vermicelli
4 eggs, separated
Pinch of salt
Caramel (either ready-made or
   homemade)
Crème Anglaise (page 164)

FOR DECORATION
Crystallized cherries
Walnuts, coarsely ground

1. Soak raisins in rum for 1 hour. Preheat oven to 180°C/350°F/Gas Mark 4.

2. In a large saucepan, heat the milk with the sugar. When it starts to boil, add vermicelli and cook for 8–10 minutes, stirring continually. Remove saucepan from heat and leave to cool.

3. Add raisins, followed by egg yolks, one at a time, beating well after each addition.

4. Beat egg whites with salt until stiff but not dry. Gently fold into vermicelli mixture.

5. Put a little caramel into the bottom of each regular-size silicone cupcake mould (about 1cm). Pour batter over caramel, filling cups ¾ full, and bake for about 15 minutes or until batter has set. Cool completely before unmoulding.

6. Cover cupcakes with Crème Anglaise, decorate with crystallized cherries and ground walnuts and serve individually.

CUPCAKE TIP
If you are making your own caramel, use sugared cubes instead of loose sugar.

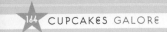

CLAFOUTIS WITH
Crème Anglaise

A clafoutis is a very rustic French dessert, somewhere between a flan and a cake.

It can be made with any fruit but a 'real' clafoutis is always made with cherries.

MAKES: ABOUT 16 REGULAR CUPCAKES OR 8 JUMBO CUPCAKES

75g ground almonds

185g plain flour

1½ teaspoons baking powder

1 teaspoon salt

125g unsalted butter, room
   temperature

200g sugar

2 eggs, slightly beaten

120ml milk

1 small shot glass cherry brandy
   (optional)

250g stoned cherries (if you
   are using frozen cherries don't
   defrost them)

Maraschino cherries for decoration

CRÈME ANGLAISE
   (VANILLA CUSTARD)

1 litre full fat milk

1 vanilla pod or 1 teaspoon vanilla
   extract

6 egg yolks

100g sugar

1. Preheat oven to 180°C/350°F/Gas Mark 4.

2. Mix almonds, flour, baking powder and salt together and set aside.

3. Cream butter and sugar until light in colour and fluffy. Add eggs, one at a time, mixing well after each addition. Alternately beat in dry ingredients and milk. Add cherry brandy. Beat batter until smooth. Fold in cherries.

4. Spoon batter into silicone cupcake moulds, filling cups about ⅔ full. Bake for 20–25 minutes or until a tester inserted into the centre comes out clean. Remove from oven, top with a maraschino cherry and cool.

5. To make Crème Angaise: bring milk and vanilla to the boil in a medium saucepan and remove from heat. Just before you are ready to use the milk, remove the vanilla pod, split it in half lengthways, and scrape out the seeds inside into the milk. Discard the pod.

6. In a large bowl, combine egg yolks and sugar and mix well. Gradually add hot milk, stirring continually. When all of the milk is used up and the mixture is smooth, return to saucepan and cook over very low heat, stirring continually. I always use a wooden spoon. The cream will thicken, little by little (do not boil). When the cream coats the back of the spoon, remove from heat and pour into another container. Stir for a few minutes to release the steam. Cool completely before serving with the clafoutis cupcakes.

CHARLOTTE À LA FRAISE Cupcakes

These are the French equivalent of strawberry shortcake and delicious, especially when strawberries are in season. Many variations exist but the following is one of my favourites since the gelatin holds the cream together and it won't fall apart when unmoulded.

MAKES: ABOUT 12 JUMBO CHARLOTTES À LA FRAISE

Flavouring (vanilla, kirsch, strawberry liqueur, etc.)
Sugar syrup (made by boiling 200g sugar with 240ml water)
500g strawberries, hulled and chopped into little pieces or coarsely crushed
200g sugar
2 teaspoons gelatin (or equivalent)
3 tablespoons cold water
3 tablespoons boiling water
1 tablespoon lemon juice
360ml whipped cream
1 package ladyfingers (I prefer the spongy ones to the dry ones because they soak up the liquid better)
Strawberry sauce (page 168) to serve

1. Add flavouring to sugar syrup. Set aside and cool.

2. In a large bowl, mix chopped or crushed strawberries and sugar.

3. In a small bowl, soak gelatin in 3 tablespoons cold water until it is soft. Add 3 tablespoons boiling water and stir until the gelatin is dissolved. Add to strawberries and mix well. Add lemon juice. When mixture starts to set, gently fold in whipped cream.

4. To assemble, quickly dip ladyfingers in cooled sugar syrup (you don't want them to be soggy) and line jumbo silicone cupcake moulds, bottom and sides, cutting to fit tightly. Fill lined moulds with strawberry cream and put in the refrigerator overnight.

5. Carefully run a dull knife around the edges and unmould on individual plates. Serve with Strawberry Sauce (page 168).

CUPCAKE TIP
You can replace the lemon juice with orange juice. Or the sugar syrup with orange juice, as for Chocolate Charlotte (page 182). This will cut the sweetness a little and the orange flavour will go well with the strawberries.

BLACK FOREST Cupcakes

The inspiration for these cupcakes, a traditional German cake, *Schwarzwälderkirschtorte*, is a mouthwatering combination of chocolate, cherries and whipped cream.

MAKES: ABOUT 16–18 REGULAR CUPCAKES OR 8 JUMBO CUPCAKES

250g plain flour
2 teaspoons baking powder
1 teaspoon salt
100g unsweetened cocoa powder
125g unsalted butter, room
   temperature
300g sugar
2 eggs
360ml milk
1 teaspoon vanilla extract
120ml kirsch or cherry brandy
   (optional but highly
   recommended!)

FILLING AND FROSTING
240ml whipping cream
200g icing sugar
½ teaspoon vanilla extract
1 tablespoon kirsch or cherry brandy
   (optional)
1 tin stoned cherries, drained
Grated dark chocolate for sprinkling

1. Preheat oven to 180°C/350°F/Gas Mark 4.

2. Mix flour, baking powder, salt and cocoa together and set aside.

3. Cream butter and sugar until light and fluffy. Add eggs, one at a time, mixing well after each addition. Alternately add flour mixture and milk. Add vanilla and beat well.

4. Spoon batter into cupcake papers, filling cups about ⅔ full. Bake for 25 minutes or until a tester inserted into the centre comes out clean. Remove from oven and cool.

5. When cupcakes are cool, unmould, cut in half or in thirds and sprinkle with cherry liqueur.

6. To make the filling and frosting: in a large bowl, whip the cream until it forms soft peaks. Add sugar, vanilla and kirsch. Beat until stiff. Spread layer(s) of cake with half the filling. Press cherries into whipped cream before adding next layer. Save enough cherries to decorate cupcakes. Frost top and sides of cupcakes with whipped cream. Decorate with remaining cherries. Sprinkle grated chocolate over cupcakes and serve individually in a pretty cupcake paper.

CUPCAKE TIP
You can replace the tinned cherries with Maraschino cherries if preferred.

CUPCAKE KEBABS

This variation on the cupcake theme is perfect for a party or for an elegant dessert, depending on the desired effect. Just about any cupcake recipe that you can use for making mini-cupcakes will do. Following are two different variations on the theme.

MAKES: ABOUT 12 KEBABS

MINI-CUPCAKES
White Fondant Glaze (page 142) or
   ready-made fondant
Food colouring (3 different ones)
Gummy sweets or fresh fruit
Bamboo skewers

STRAWBERRY SAUCE
350g strawberries
100g sugar
60ml water
A few drops lemon juice
Whipped cream for decoration

CUPCAKE TIP
*This strawberry sauce
can be kept in the
refrigerator or frozen
for later use.*

1. Follow the recipe for Lamingtons (page 178), Mini-financiers (page 110) or Genoise (page 175).

2. Either make your own fondant (see recipe for Christmas Cupcake, page 142) or use ready-made fondant, following manufacturer's instructions. Divide fondant into three bowls and put a different food colouring in each. Dip cupcakes in fondant and drain on a rack.

3. Assemble cupcakes, three to a skewer (one of each colour), alternating with the following decorations:

VARIATION: PARTY CUPCAKE KEBABS

Alternate the cupcakes with gummy sweets. Arrange the skewers attractively on a plate, surrounded by gummy sweets. These Cupcake Kebabs will be a great addition to any child's party.

VARIATION: DESSERT CUPCAKE KEBABS

Alternating the cupcakes with fresh fruit. Wash and clean the strawberries. Slowly heat the strawberries and sugar in a medium saucepan with water. When mixture starts to boil, cook for 1 minute and remove from heat. Purée by hand or in a food processor with a few drops of lemon juice. Cool before serving. Ladle a little Strawberry Sauce in a plate and lay a skewer over the sauce. Put remaining Strawberry Sauce in a bowl so that your guests can serve themselves. The idea is similar to a fondue.

ROSEMARY'S SUMMER PUDDING Cupcakes

This recipe was passed on to me by Rosemary, an Irish woman living in the south of France, who made it for me for lunch one beautiful sunny day in her village, perched between the Mediterranean and the Cevennes mountains.

MAKES: ABOUT 8 JUMBO CUPCAKES

700g summer fruits (black and
  redcurrants, cherries,
  strawberries, raspberries,
  blackberries, rhubarb, etc.)
100g sugar (to taste, depending on
  the sweetness of the fruit used)
5–6 tablespoons water
About 8–10 thin slices of white
  bread, crusts removed
Whipped cream
Mint sprigs for decoration (optional)

1. In a large saucepan, gently cook fruit, sugar and water until sugar is just melted. Fruits should hold their shape so don't overcook. Remove from heat and cool slightly.

2. Cut rounds of white bread to fit the bottom of jumbo silicone cupcake moulds. Cut bread to line the sides. You want the entire inside of the mould to be covered, fitting the bread neatly together. Carefully scoop fruit into lined cupcakes, saving a little of the juice. Cut the remaining bread to form a lid and cover the fruit, pressing the bread into the fruit so that it absorbs the liquid. Cover with aluminium foil and place in the refrigerator overnight.

3. When ready to serve, invert onto a serving dish and pour a little of the reserved liquid over each cupcake. The fruit will have completely saturated the bread and it will be a wonderful dark purple colour. Serve with whipped cream and a sprig of mint.

CUPCAKE TIP
I have found that frozen berry mixtures work particularly well.

CHOC & NUT Dacquoise

A 'Dacquoise' is a classic French pastry of baked nut meringues layered with butter cream. Here, the meringue is made with almonds and hazelnuts with a chocolate ganache filling.

1. Make the meringues following Almond and Hazelnut Mini-Meringues (page 150), using regular silicone moulds instead of mini-cupcake moulds. Put about 1cm of the uncooked meringue in the bottom of a mould. (You can also trace circles the diameter of a cupcake on a piece of wax paper. Turn the paper over, place it on a rigid ovenproof dish and pipe or spread meringue over the circle, about 1cm thick.)

2. Bake until meringue is golden brown and firm to the touch. Wait until it has entirely cooled to unmould.

3. To make the ganache: place chocolate and cream in a bowl set over a saucepan of simmering water and heat until cream is warm to the touch and the chocolate starts to melt (do not boil). Remove from heat and stir until all of the chocolate has melted and the mixture is homogeneous. Place bowl in cold water. When chocolate is cool to the touch, beat ganache for about 10 minutes with an electric beater until the colour lightens and soft shiny peaks form.

4. To assemble: when the disks are cool, line a cupcake mould with pretty cupcake papers. Place a disk in the bottom of each cupcake paper. Spread or pipe a layer of ganache over the disk and place a second disk on top, lightly pressing it into the ganache. Cover the cupcake tin with clingfilm and put it in the refrigerator for at least 2 hours until the ganache has set. Dust with icing sugar before serving.

MAKES: ABOUT 10 CUPCAKES

Almond and Hazelnut Meringues
  (page 150)
WHIPPED CHOCOLATE GANACHE
180g dark chocolate, broken into
  little pieces
180ml double cream
Icing sugar for dusting

CUPCAKE TIP
You can also assemble these cupcakes in silicone moulds without cupcake papers or in no mould at all.

GELÉE OF FRUIT WITH WHITE WINE IN A Cupcake

This surprising dessert lends itself well to a cupcake format. Basically, it is a fruit salad in white wine jelly, an ideal and elegant dessert for any season, depending on the fruit that is available. It will be a perfect and light ending to a gourmet meal.

MAKES: ABOUT 12 REGULAR CUPCAKES OR 6 JUMBO CUPCAKES

500g of fresh fruit, washed and cut into small pieces (pears, cherries, strawberries, bananas, pineapple, peaches, apricots, oranges, apples, etc.)
1 heaped tablespoon unflavoured gelatin (or equivalent)
240ml water
100g sugar
240ml dry white wine
1 tablespoon lemon juice

1. Prepare fruits. Place fruits on a paper towel or a clean dish towel to absorb extra moisture.

2. Dissolve gelatin in 120ml water in a bowl over a pan of simmering water. After it has dissolved, remove it from the heat but keep over hot water.

3. In a large bowl, mix remaining water, sugar, wine and lemon juice. Stir with a whisk until all of the sugar has dissolved. Add gelatin and continue stirring. Pour 5mm of the liquid into each cup of a silicone cupcake mould (either regular or jumbo). Put mould in refrigerator until gelatin has set (about 1 hour).

4. Remove from refrigerator and fill cups with mixed fruits. Pour remaining gelatin mixture over fruits, covering them with 5mm of the liquid. Put mould back in the refrigerator for at least 6 hours.

5. To unmould, run a dull knife (very carefully!) around the edges of the mould and unmould onto a serving platter. Keep in the refrigerator until you are ready to serve.

DESSERT
Cups

Dessert Cups are hard chocolate cups made in a cupcake paper. They can be made with dark chocolate, milk chocolate or white chocolate. The white chocolate cups are wonderful filled with fresh berries and the dark cups are delicious with raspberries. Fill any of them with candy for a party and set them in pretty cupcake papers.

MAKES: ABOUT 12 CUPS

425g white chocolate
350g fresh or defrosted frozen berries
   (raspberries, strawberries, etc.)
Sugar to taste
Raspberry sauce (see page 96)
Whipped cream (optional)

1. Melt the chocolate in a bowl set over a saucepan of simmering water or in a microwave.

2. Using a pastry brush, coat inside of a cupcake paper set in a muffin tin with melted chocolate (chocolate should be cool to the touch but of good spreading consistency). Put muffin tin in the refrigerator for about 20 minutes or until chocolate has hardened. Take it out of the refrigerator and add another coat. You may need to set chocolate over warm water or put it back in the microwave again to get it to the right consistency. Put cups back in refrigerator again so that the chocolate can harden. If you want sturdier cups, add a third coat.

3. When the cups are hard, peel off paper very carefully. You can keep these cups in a cool dry place or freeze them for future use.

4. Fill cups with berries, sprinkle with sugar and drizzle with raspberry sauce. Add a dollop of whipped cream, if desired.

SPECIAL OCCASION
Cupcakes

These cupcakes are perfect for special occasions such as birthdays, weddings, graduations or showers. The principle is that they are made of two cupcakes made in a silicone mould – a regular size and a mini-size – assembled, frosted with fondant and decorated for the occasion, whatever it may be.

MAKES: **10 REGULAR AND 10 MINI-CUPCAKES**

GENOISE CUPCAKE
250g sugar
6 eggs
250g plain flour
125g unsalted butter, melted and slightly cooled (but still warm to the touch)
Flavouring (vanilla, almond extract, etc.)
FOOD COLOURING (OPTIONAL)
White Fondant Glaze (page 142)

1. Preheat oven to 180°C/350°F/Gas Mark 4.

2. Put sugar and eggs in a bowl set over a saucepan of simmering water. Using a whisk or a hand-held beater (electric or otherwise), beat mixture constantly as it heats until it is lemony in colour and forms soft peaks. The whole procedure should take about 10–15 minutes. Remove from heat and very gently fold in the flour, butter and flavouring with a whisk.

3. Carefully spoon batter into regular and mini-silicone moulds (you will need the same number of each), filling about ⅔ full. Bake for about 20 minutes, a shorter time for the mini-cupcakes, or until a tester inserted into the centre comes out clean and cupcakes are just slightly golden on top. Remove from oven and cool.

4. Add food colouring to the fondant, depending on occasion. (For instance, you can use red and/or blue food colouring for a baby shower.) Set some of the fondant aside for dipping the mini-cupcakes.

5. To assemble: ice cooled regular-size cupcakes with fondant. Dip mini-cupcakes in the fondant and place on top of regular cupcakes. Decorate.

FAR BRETON
Cupcakes

A Far Breton is a speciality from Brittany, in the Celtic northwest corner of France. It is a rather rustic flan, made with prunes, a perfect dessert for winter when fresh fruits are rare. I suggest making these cupcakes in a silicone cupcake mould so that they can be easily unmoulded and served luke warm with Vanilla Custard flavoured with a little rum.

MAKES: ABOUT 12 CUPCAKES

12 stoned prunes
1 small glass of rum for soaking
   prunes (about 60ml)
115g plain flour
Pinch of salt
100g sugar
2 eggs, slightly beaten
360ml full fat milk
65g unsalted butter, melted and
   cooled
Icing sugar for dusting
Vanilla custard (page 164) to serve

1. In a bowl, soak prunes in rum for about an hour, turning from time to time. Drain liquid and save. Set prunes aside.

2. Preheat oven to 180°C/350°F/Gas Mark 4.

3. In a large bowl, mix the flour, salt and sugar. Beat eggs with milk and butter and add liquid to dry ingredients, mixing well with a wooden spoon or an electric mixer. Batter will be liquid. Stir in 2 tablespoons of the liquid from the prunes.

4. Place a prune in each cup of a regular silicone cupcake mould and fill just ½ full. Cook for about 35 minutes or until brown on top. Batter will rise and then deflate when it cools. Remove from oven and leave to cool.

5. Sprinkle with icing sugar and serve on a plate with Vanilla Custard (page 164) to which you have added a little of the rum used for soaking the prunes.

CUPCAKE TIP
*Alternatively,
just serve them in a
pretty cupcake paper
dusted with icing sugar.*

LAMINGTON
Mini-Cupcakes

A Lamington is a small square of plain white cake or sponge cake, dipped in melted chocolate and sugar and coated with desiccated coconut. It is a speciality of Australia.

MAKES: ABOUT 40 MINI-CUPCAKES

300g plain flour
2 teaspoons baking powder
1 teaspoon salt
125g unsalted butter, room temperature
150g sugar
2 eggs
1 teaspoon vanilla extract
120ml milk
300g desiccated coconut, toasted for extra flavour

CHOCOLATE ICING
3 tablespoons boiling water
1 tablespoon unsalted butter
35g unsweetened cocoa powder
300g icing sugar

1. Preheat oven to 180°C/350°F/Gas Mark 4. Mix flour, baking powder and salt and set aside.

2. Cream butter and sugar together until light and fluffy. Add eggs, one at a time, mixing well after each addition. Blend in vanilla. Alternately add flour mixture and milk and beat until batter is smooth.

3. Spoon batter into silicone mini-cupcake moulds, a heaped teaspoon of batter per mini-cupcake. Cook for about 15 minutes or until brown on top. Remove from oven and cool.

4. Spread out coconut on a piece of wax paper or in a large shallow bowl and set aside.

5. To make the icing: pour boiling water over butter. Add cocoa and mix well. Gradually add sugar and beat until mixture is smooth with a whisk or a wooden spoon. The chocolate should be smooth and glossy (it should also be thin enough to easily cover the cupcakes – add extra boiling water if necessary).

6. Using two forks or prongs, dip the cupcakes into the chocolate and roll in the coconut. Set cupcakes on a cake rack until they have cooled. These cupcakes freeze well.

PARTY SUNDAE Cupcakes

Serve these cupcakes as you would a sundae, in an ice cream dish, with all the trimmings. I have given a recipe for Hot Fudge Sauce but you can use any sauce you wish.

MAKES: 16 CUPCAKES

VANILLA PEANUT CUPCAKE
300g plain flour
2 teaspoons baking powder
125g unsalted butter, room
   temperature
120g soft light brown sugar
2 eggs
1 teaspoon vanilla extract
180ml milk
60g coarsely chopped salted peanuts

HOT FUDGE SAUCE
240ml whipping cream
60ml golden syrup
360g good quality chocolate (at least
   55% cocoa solids)
65g unsalted butter, room
   temperature
1 teaspoon vanilla extract
Ice cream of your choice
Chopped peanuts, whipped cream
   and Maraschino cherries for
   decoration

1. Preheat oven to 180°C/350°F/Gas Mark 4.

2. Mix flour and baking powder together and set aside.

3. Cream butter and sugar until light and fluffy. Add eggs, one at a time, mixing well after each addition. Alternately beat in flour mixture, milk and vanilla extract. Fold in peanuts.

4. Spoon batter into regular silicone cupcake moulds, filling about ⅔ full. Bake for 20–25 minutes or until a tester inserted in the centre comes out clean. Remove from oven and cool.

5. To make the sauce: in a saucepan, slowly heat cream, golden syrup and chocolate, stirring constantly. Simmer for 5–10 minutes or until mixture starts to thicken. Remove from heat and stir in butter and vanilla. Cool slightly before using. You can keep this sauce in the refrigerator and gently reheat it before using.

6. Using a sharp knife, cut a wide shallow hole in the top of each cupcake, the width of a scoop of ice cream, and just deep enough to hold it. Put cupcake in an ice cream dish, fill with a scoop of ice cream and pour the fudge sauce over the cupcake. Top with chopped peanuts, whipped cream and a maraschino cherry.

OPERA Cupcakes

An 'Opera' is a traditional French pastry found in the finest pastry shops across France. It is not difficult to make but requires a bit of time and patience. The traditional cake usually comes in the form of a layered sheet cake cut into rectangles. A true 'Opera' will have a little piece of gold leaf (edible, of course) on top. This is a somewhat simplified version.

MAKES: **ABOUT 12 REGULAR CUPCAKES OR 6 JUMBO CUPCAKES**

GIOCONDA BISCUIT (BISCUIT JOCONDE) — THE TRADITIONAL CAKE RECIPE USED TO MAKE THE PASTRY):

65g unsalted butter

125g finely ground almonds

130g sugar, plus 2 tablespoons

35g plain flour

4 eggs, separated

Pinch of salt

Chocolate Ganache (page 171) made using 120g chocolate and 120ml double cream

½ quantity Mocha Butter Cream Frosting (page 70)

Edible gold leaf or glitter sugar for decoration

1. Preheat oven to 130°C/250°F/Gas Mark ½.

2. Melt butter and set aside until cool.

3. Beat almonds, 130g sugar, flour and egg yolks until the mixture is light and foamy (at least 10 minutes).

4. In a separate bowl, beat egg whites with salt and remaining sugar until they are stiff but not dry. Gently fold into almond mixture. Delicately add cooled melted butter, using a spatula or a whisk.

5. Fill silicone cupcake moulds just a little over half way. Bake for about 10 minutes or until brown on top. Be careful not to burn these cupcakes — they will cook quickly.

6. Unmould when cupcakes are cool and cut into three equal layers.

7. Beat half of the ganache with an electric beater for about 5–10 minutes until it is light and fluffy. If the other half hardens before you can use it, set it over warm water until it is of the right consistency.

8. To assemble, spread Mocha Buttercream Icing on the first layer. Add second layer and spread beaten Chocolate Ganache. Add third layer and ice with liquid ganache. Decorate with a piece of edible gold leaf or glitter sugar and serve in pretty cupcake papers.

CHOCOLATE CHARLOTTE Cupcakes

When I had my restaurant in the south of France, Chocolate Charlotte was by far the most popular dessert we made and I had to make one every day or my customers would go away disappointed. This is the cupcake version of that very charlotte.

MAKES: ABOUT 8–10 JUMBO CUPCAKES

240g dark chocolate
125g unsalted butter, cut into small
   pieces
100g sugar
3 eggs, separated
120ml whipping cream
Pinch of salt
1 package ladyfingers (I prefer the
   spongy ones to the dry ones
   because they soak up the liquid
   better)
Orange juice

FOR DECORATION
Custard or Raspberry Sauce (page 96)
Roses and extra chocolate sauce

1. Melt chocolate, butter and sugar in a bowl set over a saucepan of simmering water until chocolate is just melted. Remove from heat immediately and add egg yolks, one at a time, beating well after each addition. Set mixture aside and leave to cool. When mixture is cool, pour in cream. The mixture will seize up a bit and thicken.

2. Beat egg whites with a pinch of salt until stiff but not dry. Gently fold into chocolate mixture.

3. To assemble, briefly dip ladyfingers in orange juice – you don't want them to be soggy. Line the sides of the jumbo silicone cupcake moulds, cutting ladyfingers to size and squeezing them together tightly. Fill lined moulds with chocolate mixture to just a little below the top. Cover cupcakes with more ladyfingers dipped in orange juice, fitting them well to cover all of the chocolate. Place mould in refrigerator overnight.

4. Unmould onto a serving dish and serve upside down, either in a pretty cupcake paper or on a plate with custard and/or Raspberry Sauce (page 96).

AUNT FLORENCE'S FROZEN LEMON Cupcakes

This recipe comes to me from my cousin Deborah (via her cousin Jocelyn) whose mother (my Aunt Florence) used to make them for her as a special treat. Deborah tells me that she used to make them as well until she realized how bad whipping cream was for the health. So throw caution to the wind and make these very easy and elegant cupcakes for that special occasion.

MAKES: ABOUT 12 CUPCAKES

LEMON CREAM
200g sugar
Juice and finely grated rind of
    1 lemon
480ml whipping cream

CRUST
125g unsalted butter, room
    temperature
75g crushed digestive biscuits
75g crushed corn flakes
2 tablespoons sugar
Jellied lemon slices for decoration

1. To make the lemon cream: combine sugar and lemon juice and rind in a large bowl. Gradually beat in cream.

2. To make the crust: melt butter in a saucepan over low heat and stir in crushed digestive biscuits, corn flakes and sugar.

3. Place crust mixture in the bottom of cupcake moulds. Pour lemon cream on top. Freeze for at least 3 hours. Unmould, top with a jellied lemon slice and serve.

CUPCAKE TIP
You can use cupcake papers or make these frozen cupcakes in either a rigid or a silicone mould.

INDEX

A

after eight cupcakes 81

almonds

almond & hazelnut mini-meringues 150

almond butter cream frosting 121

the Arlésienne 94

Bourdaloue cupcakes 87

cherry almond pie cupcakes 154

choc & nut Dacquoise 171

clafoutis with crème Anglais 164

courgette pine nut cupcakes 18

Epiphany cupcakes 121

linzertorte cupcakes 102

mendiant cupcakes 103

mini-financier cupcakes 110

opera cupcakes 181

Orient Express cupcakes 108

saffron & orange cupcakes 115

American parfait icing 130

anise butter cream frosting 78

apples

apple-cranberry crumble cupcakes 28

caramelized apples 84

deep-dish apple pie cupcakes 151

strudel cups 161

tarte tatin cupcakes 84

Thanksgiving apple cider cupcakes 134

apricots 94

Arlésienne, the 94

Aunt Florence's frozen lemon cupcakes 185

B

baba au rhum cupcakes 158

baking tips 11

Baklava cups 155

banana split cupcakes 56

beer & peanuts cupcakes 65

birthday beauties 46

black & white cupcakes 20

blackcurrants

Kir cupcakes 66

Rosemary's summer pudding cupcakes 170

Black Forest cupcakes 167

blackberries 170

blueberries

blue blueberry 'n' cream cupcakes 22

blueberry tart cupcakes 159

July 4th blueberry & raspberry cupcakes 132

Boston cream cupcakes 162

bourbon 71

Bourdaloue cupcakes 87

brandy

   Christmas fruit cupcakes 142

   midnight madness cupcakes 76

brownie cupcakes 24

Burgundy blues cupcakes 62

butter rum frosting 64

C

cappuccino cupcakes 68

caramel vermicelli cupcake flans 163

caramelized apples 84

carrots 133

Cevenol cupcakes 88

champagne 144

Chanukah honey hazelnut cupcakes 140

Charlotte à la fraise cupcakes 166

cherries

   Black Forest cupcakes 167

   cherry almond pie cupcakes 154

clafoutis with crème Anglais 164

pineapple surprises 106

Rosemary's summer pudding cupcakes 170

Valentine's Day cupcakes 120

chestnuts 88

chocolate

   after eight cupcakes 81

   basic chocolate cupcakes 52

   birthday beauties 46

   black & white cupcakes 20

   Black Forest cupcakes 167

   brownie cupcakes 24

   Burgundy blues cupcakes 62

   choc & nut Dacquoise 171

   chocolate & peanut butter cupcakes 25

   chocolate charlotte cupcakes 182

   chocolate coconut cupcakes 19

   chocolate cupcake pies 152

   chocolate fudge frosting 56

   chocolate ganache 81

   chocolate hazelnut cupcakes 44

   chocolate malted milk shake cupcakes 58

chocolate mousse cupcakes 90

chocolate sundae cupcakes 48

Christmas peppermint chocolate cupcakes 141

cookies 'n' cream cupcakes 49

Day of the Dead choc cinnamon cupcakes 138

dessert cups 174

dessert rose cupcakes 148

Earl Grey cupcakes 92

hot chocolate & marshmallows cupcakes 50

July 4th red velvet cupcakes 130

lamington mini cupcakes 178

macadamia & white chocolate cupcakes 107

Marrakech moments 104

mezzo-mezzo cupcakes 72

midnight madness cupcakes 76

mint julep cupcakes 71

opera cupcakes 181

Poire Belle Hélène 111

rocky road cupcakes 54

s'mores cupcakes 57

Valentine's Day cupcakes 120

white chocolate & raspberry
cupcakes 112
white chocolate panna cotta
cupcakes 156
Christmas fruit cupcakes 142
Christmas peppermint chocolate
cupcakes 141
cider 134
cinnamon and spice frosting 133
cinnamon butter frosting 138
clafoutis with crème Anglaise 164
coconut
chocolate coconut cupcakes 19
lamington mini cupcakes 178
Piña Colada cupcakes 77
pineapple surprises 106
Yeti cupcakes 42

coffee
cappuccino cupcakes 68
Irish coffee cupcakes 70
mezzo-mezzo cupcakes 72
tiramisu cupcakes 101
cookies 'n' cream cupcakes 49
courgette pine nut cupcakes 18
cranberries
apple-cranberry crumble
cupcakes 28
Thanksgiving carrot & cranberry
cupcakes 133
cream cheese frosting 18
cream chocolate sauce 111
crème Anglaise 164
crème brûlée cupcakes 93
Crêpe Suzette cupcakes 89
Cuba Libre cupcakes 69
cupcake papers 13
cupcake tins 12
cupcake kebabs 168
currants 124

D
Day of the Dead choc cinnamon
cupcakes 138

decorations 14–15
deep-dish apple pie cupcakes 151
dessert cups 174
dessert rose cupcakes 148
digestive biscuit and milk
chocolate cupcakes 57

E
Earl Grey cupcakes 92
Easter lavender butterfly
cupcakes 129
Easter lemon chiffon cupcakes 126
Epiphany cupcakes 121
equipment 12–13

F
Far Breton cupcakes 176
figs
the Languedocienne 98
mendiant cupcakes 103
frosting 14–15
fruit
dessert cups 174
fruit yogurt cupcakes 36
gelée of fruit with white wine in
a cupcake 172

Rosemary's summer pudding
cupcakes 170

see also apples etc

G

gateau de Savoie 114

gelée of fruit with white wine in a
cupcake 172

Genoise cupcakes 175

ginger 30

glazes 14–15

goat cheese frosting 98

grapefruit 38

green tea cupcakes 108

H

Halloween orange juice
cupcakes 136

Halloween pumpkin pecan
cupcakes 137

hazelnuts
almond & hazelnut mini-
meringues 150
Chanukah honey hazelnut
cupcakes 140
choc & nut Dacquoise 171

chocolate hazelnut cupcakes 44

linzertorte cupcakes 102

mendiant cupcakes 103

honey
Baklava cups 155
Chanukah honey hazelnut
cupcakes 140
the Languedocienne 98
poppyseed & lavender honey
cupcakes 37

hot chocolate & marshmallows
cupcakes 50

hot fudge sauce 180

I

icing 14–15

ingredients 10–11

Irish coffee cupcakes 70

J

jam
the Arlésienne 94
Christmas fruit cupcakes 142
Easter lavender butterfly
cupcakes 129
jam-filled cupcakes 52

Kir cupcakes 66

mini-financier cupcakes 110

Mother's Day filled rose
cupcakes 125

peanut butter & jam swirls 53

strawberry & rhubarb crisp
cupcakes 34

strawberry-filled oatmeal
cupcakes 32

July 4th blueberry & raspberry
cupcakes 132

July 4th red velvet cupcakes 130

K

Kir cupcakes 66

L

lamington mini cupcakes 178

Languedocienne, the 98

lemons
Aunt Florence's frozen lemon
cupcakes 185
birthday beauties 46
Christmas fruit cupcakes 142
Easter lavender butterfly
cupcakes 129

Easter lemon chiffon
    cupcakes 126
lemon meringue pie cupcakes 26
sunshine & vitamin C
    cupcakes 38
limes
    margarita cupcakes 75
    ricotta lime cupcakes 99
linzertorte cupcakes 102

M

macadamia nuts 107
maple syrup 29
margarita cupcakes 75
Marrakech moments 104
marsala 101
marshmallows
    hot chocolate & marshmallow
        cupcakes 50

rocky road cupcakes 54
s'mores cupcakes 57
Yeti cupcakes 42
mascarpone cream 101
mendiant cupcakes 103
mezzo-mezzo cupcakes 72
midnight madness
    cupcakes 76
mini-financier cupcakes 110
mint
    after eight cupcakes 81
    mint julep cupcakes 71
mocha butter cream frosting 70
Mother's Day filled rose
    cupcakes 125

N

New Year's Eve confetti
    cupcakes 145
New Year's Eve pink champagne
    cupcakes 144
no-cook marshmallow icing 57
nuts
    Baklava cups 155
    persimmon nut harvest treat 33
    see also almonds etc

O

oatmeal
    St. Patrick's Day Irish soda bread
        cupcakes 124
    strawberry-filled oatmeal
        cupcakes 32
old-fashioned fudge frosting 48
opera cupcakes 181
oranges
    Christmas fruit cupcakes 142
    Crepe Suzette cupcakes 89
    Halloween orange juice
        cupcakes 136
    Marrakech moments 104
    orange cream cheese frosting 33
    saffron & orange cupcakes 115
    sunshine & vitamin C
        cupcakes 38
Orient Express cupcakes 108

P

papers, for cupcakes 13
party sundae cupcakes 180
passion fruit 156
pastel cupcake frosting 46
pastis cupcakes 78

peaches 96

peanut butter

   chocolate & peanut butter

     cupcakes 25

   peanut butter & jam

     swirls 53

peanuts

   beer & peanuts cupcakes 65

   party sundae cupcakes 180

pears

   Bourdaloue cupcakes 87

   Poire Belle Hélène 111

pecan nuts 137

pêche melba cupcakes 96

peppermint 141

persimmon nut harvest treats 33

Piña Colada cupcakes 77

pine nuts 18

pineapple

Piña Colada cupcakes 77

pineapple surprises 106

pistachio nuts

   mini-financier cupcakes 110

   St. Patrick's Day pistachio yogurt

     cupcakes 122

Poire Belle Hélène 111

poppyseed & lavender honey

   cupcakes 37

prunes 176

pumpkin 137

R

raisins

   mendiant cupcakes 103

   rum raisin cupcakes 64

   St. Patrick's Day Irish soda bread

     cupcakes 124

   strudel cups 161

raspberries

   the Arlésienne 94

   July 4th blueberry & raspberry

     cupcakes 132

   pêche melba cupcakes 96

   Rosemary's summer pudding

     cupcakes 170

   white chocolate & raspberry

     cupcakes 112

real vanilla cupcakes 48

red currants 170

rhubarb

   Rosemary's summer pudding

     cupcakes 170

   strawberry & rhubarb crisp

     cupcakes 34

ricotta lime cupcakes 99

rocky road cupcakes 54

root beer float 45

rose syrup 125

Rosemary's summer pudding

   cupcakes 170

rum

   baba au rhum cupcakes 158

   Cuba Libre cupcakes 69

   midnight madness cupcakes 76

   Piña Colada cupcakes 77

   rum raisin cupcakes 64

S

saffron & orange cupcakes 115

Savoy cake 114

s'mores cupcakes 57

snow frosting 42

special occasion cupcakes
175

St. Patrick's Day Irish soda
bread cupcakes 124

St. Patrick's Day pistachio yogurt
cupcakes 122

steamed coffee frosting 68

strawberries
birthday beauties 46

Charlotte à la fraise
cupcakes 166

cupcake kebabs 168

strawberry & rhubarb crisp
cupcakes 34

strawberry cheesecake 116

strudel cups 161

sunshine & vitamin C cupcakes 38

T

tarte tatin cupcakes 84

tea
Christmas peppermint chocolate
cupcakes 141

Earl Grey cupcakes 92

Orient Express cupcakes 108

tequila 75

Thanksgiving apple cider
cupcakes 134

Thanksgiving carrot & cranberry
cupcakes 133

three citrus fruit custard 38

three-gingerbread cupcake 30

tins, for cupcakes 12

tiramisu cupcakes 101

toppings 14–15

V

Valentine's Day cupcakes 120

vanilla cupcakes, real 48

vermicelli 163

W

walnuts
brownie cupcakes 24

maple walnut delight 29

rocky road cupcakes 54

strudel cups 161

Thanksgiving carrot & cranberry
cupcakes 133

whiskey
Irish coffee cupcakes 70

St. Patrick's Day Irish soda bread
cupcakes 124

white chocolate
white chocolate & raspberry
cupcakes 112

white chocolate cream cheese
frosting 48

white chocolate mint
frosting 71

white chocolate panna cotta
cupcakes 156

white velvet cupcakes 42

Y

yellow cupcakes, basic 52

Yeti cupcakes 42

'yin-yang' frosting 108

yogurt cupcakes 36